BUSINESS ISSUES, COMPETITION AND ENTREPRENEURSHIP

PENSION ADVANCE COMPANIES

QUESTIONABLE BUSINESS PRACTICES

Business Issues, Competition and Entrepreneurship

Additional books in this series can be found on Nova's website under the Series tab.

Additional e-books in this series can be found on Nova's website under the e-book tab.

BUSINESS ISSUES, COMPETITION AND ENTREPRENEURSHIP

PENSION ADVANCE COMPANIES

QUESTIONABLE BUSINESS PRACTICES

CASSIDY L. WALLER
EDITOR

New York

For permission to use material from this book please contact us:
Telephone 631-231-7269; Fax 631-231-8175
Web Site: http://www.novapublishers.com

Library of Congress Cataloging-in-Publication Data

ISBN: 978-1-63463-539-4

Published by Nova Science Publishers, Inc. † New York

CONTENTS

PREFACE

Pension advances and pension investments are products that, while based on or related to pension benefits, are generally distinct from the pensions themselves. A pension advance is an up-front lump sum provided to a consumer in exchange for a certain number and dollar amount of the consumer's future pension payments plus various fees. Pension investments, the related product, provide investors a future income stream when they make an up-front lump-sum investment in one or more pensioners' incomes. There have been recent concerns about companies attempting to take advantage of retirees using pension advances. This book describes the number and characteristics of pension advance companies and marketing practices; evaluates how pension advance terms compare with those of other products; and evaluates the extent to which there is related federal oversight.

Chapter 1 – There have been recent concerns about companies attempting to take advantage of retirees using pension advances. GAO was asked to review business practices related to pension advances. This report (1) describes the number and characteristics of pension advance companies and marketing practices; (2) evaluates how pension advance terms compare with those of other products; and (3) evaluates the extent to which there is related federal oversight. GAO identified 38 pension advance companies and related marketing practices using company websites and nonpublic databases. GAO conducted a more-detailed nongeneralizable assessment of 19 of these companies selected based on factors such as marketing claims and presence of or lack of complaints. GAO used undercover investigative phone calls to identify additional marketing practices and to obtain pension advance offers. This information was compared with the terms of other financial products, such as personal loans. GAO also examined the role of selected federal agencies with oversight of consumer protection and pension issues.

Chapter 2 – Report of the Federal Trade Commission on Pension Advances: Not So Fast.

Chapter 3 – Report of the U.S. Securities and Exchange Commission on Pension or Settlement Income Streams: What You Need to Know Before Buying or Selling Them.

In: Pension Advance Companies
Editor: Cassidy L. Waller
ISBN: 978-1-63463-539-4

Chapter 1

PENSION ADVANCE TRANSACTIONS: QUESTIONABLE BUSINESS PRACTICES IDENTIFIED*

United States Government Accountability Office

WHY GAO DID THIS STUDY

There have been recent concerns about companies attempting to take advantage of retirees using pension advances. GAO was asked to review business practices related to pension advances. This report (1) describes the number and characteristics of pension advance companies and marketing practices; (2) evaluates how pension advance terms compare with those of other products; and (3) evaluates the extent to which there is related federal oversight. GAO identified 38 pension advance companies and related marketing practices using company websites and nonpublic databases. GAO conducted a more-detailed nongeneralizable assessment of 19 of these companies selected based on factors such as marketing claims and presence of or lack of complaints. GAO used undercover investigative phone calls to identify additional marketing practices and to obtain pension advance offers. This information was compared with the terms of other financial products,

---

* This is an edited, reformatted and augmented version of a United States Government Accountability Office publication, No. GAO-14-420, dated June 2014.

such as personal loans. GAO also examined the role of selected federal agencies with oversight of consumer protection and pension issues.

What GAO Recommends

GAO recommends that CFPB and FTC review the pension advance practices identified in this report and exercise oversight or enforcement as appropriate. GAO also recommends that CFPB coordinate with relevant agencies to increase consumer education about pension advances. CFPB and FTC agreed with GAO's recommendations.

What GAO Found

\GAO identified at least 38 companies that offered individuals lump-sum payments or "advances" in exchange for receiving part or all of their pension payment streams. Eighteen of these companies were concentrated in one state, and 17 offered a range of other financial products in addition to pension advances. The 38 companies used multistep pension advance processes that included various other parties. At least 21 of the 38 companies were affiliated with each other in ways that were not apparent to consumers. All of the companies operated primarily as web-based companies, and some targeted financially vulnerable consumers with poor or bad credit nationwide. GAO received offers from 6 out of 19 pension advance companies. These offers did not compare favorably with other financial products or offerings, such as loans and lump-sum options through pension plans. For example, the effective interest rates on pension advances offered to GAO during its undercover investigation typically ranged from approximately 27 percent to 46 percent, which were at times close to two to three times higher than the legal limits set by the related states on the interest rates assessed for various types of personal credit.

GAO identified questionable elements of pension advance transactions related to the disclosure of rates or fees, and certain unfavorable terms of agreements. The Bureau of Consumer Financial Protection (CFPB) and Federal Trade Commission (FTC) have oversight responsibility over certain acts and practices that may harm consumers. According to CFPB officials, CFPB's oversight has been limited to instances where products met certain characteristics. FTC officials stated that FTC has not taken any public enforcement actions because it has not received many complaints, among other reasons. Six other federal agencies have oversight over pensions and provide related education. These agencies provided limited consumer education regarding pension advance transactions, but almost all agreed that it would be beneficial. Consumers who are vulnerable to financial exploitation may lack the information needed to make sound decisions. CFPB facilitates coordinating federal financial education and could help ensure information reaches relevant pensioners.

ABBREVIATIONS

1933 Act	Securities Act of 1933
1934 Act	Securities Exchange Act of 1934
CFPB	Bureau of Consumer Financial Protection
DOD	Department of Defense
Dodd-Frank Act	Dodd-Frank Wall Street Reform and Consumer Protection Act of 2010
DOL	Department of Labor
EBSA	Employee Benefits Security Administration
ERISA	Employee Retirement Income Security Act of 1974
FINRA	Financial Industry Regulatory Authority
FTC	Federal Trade Commission
FTC Act	Federal Trade Commission Act
IRS	Internal Revenue Service
NCLC	National Consumer Law Center
OPM	Office of Personnel Management
PBGC	Pension Benefit Guaranty Corporation
SEC	Securities and Exchange Commission
TILA	Truth in Lending Act
Treasury	Department of the Treasury
UDAP	Unfair and Deceptive Acts and Practices
VA	Department of Veterans Affairs

June 4, 2014

The Honorable Tom Harkin
Chairman
The Honorable Lamar Alexander
Ranking Member
Committee on Health, Education, Labor, and Pensions
United States Senate

Pensions are the foundation of economic security in retirement for millions of middle-class families and play a critical role in ensuring financial security at retirement. During an individual's retirement years, pensions are often the key source of income that allows the retiree, along with Social Security, to maintain a reasonable standard of living. Thus, a partial loss of pension benefits can significantly affect a retiree's ability to pay monthly living expenses, medical bills, or other unexpected expenses. Recent media coverage has highlighted marketing efforts of companies to encourage borrowing against pensions—generally referred to as pension advances—and has indicated that some companies may be attempting to take advantage of financially distressed retirees who are in immediate need of a large sum of cash.[1]

In 2010, the U.S. Census Bureau reported that the number of Americans age 65 and older is projected to more than double over the next 40 years, reaching almost 89 million in 2050. Also, a 2011 study by the MetLife Mature Market Institute on elder financial abuse reported that older Americans lose an estimated $2.9 billion annually to financial exploitation when factoring in estimated unreported losses.[2] These statistics highlight that the elderly population will grow significantly in the next few decades as well as concerns about the population's vulnerability to abuse and related financial exploitation. The Federal Trade Commission (FTC), Bureau of Consumer Financial Protection, commonly known as the Consumer Financial Protection Bureau (CFPB), and Securities and Exchange Commission (SEC) may have consumer protection and investor oversight roles or other responsibilities related to pension advances depending on a number of factors, including whether the transaction involves consumer financial products and services, other consumer products or services, or investment products; or depending on the provider of the service. The Department of Labor's (DOL) Employee Benefits Security Administration (EBSA), Department of the Treasury (Treasury), Pension Benefit Guaranty Corporation (PBGC), Office of Personnel Management

(OPM), and Departments of Defense (DOD) and Veterans Affairs (VA) may also have pension oversight roles depending on whether the pensioner was a private-sector employee, a federal government civilian worker (hereafter referred to as a federal pensioner), or a military veteran.[3]

You asked us to examine entities marketing these financial products and to provide case-study examples of the practices that are used, and to review federal and state laws and regulations that may be applicable. This report (1) describes the number and characteristics of entities offering pension advances and the marketing practices that pension advance companies employ, (2) evaluates how pension advance terms compare with those of other financial products, and (3) evaluates the extent to which there are federal oversight mechanisms in place related to pension advances.[4]

To describe the number and characteristics of entities offering pension advances and the marketing practices that pension advance companies employ, we identified companies that offer pension advances by performing a comprehensive search of companies that market these products to consumers online, reviewing newspaper and magazine articles, conducting queries of federal and public databases that capture information on companies, and interviewing officials from agencies and organizations that provide information to and collect information from retired consumers.[5] Pension advance transactions have two major components: the up-front lump-sum payment provided to consumers in exchange for a certain number (and dollar amount) of the consumer's future pension payments (known as the pension advance) and the pension stream payments provided to investors in exchange for providing the lump sum (known as the pension investment).[6] For purposes of this report, we focused more on the pension advance component than on the pension investment component in order to highlight the direct effect on pensioners. For the 38 companies that we identified as having offered pension advance products, we obtained demographic information using public and nonpublic data.[7] We also obtained additional data on 19 of the 38 pension advance companies selected for case studies, which we use for illustrative examples in this report. These 19 companies were selected based on factors such as varying types of marketing claims, presence of or lack of consumer complaints, and varying size of business.[8] For these 19 selected companies, we conducted undercover investigative phone calls, submitted online quote requests for pension advances, or obtained documentation directly from the companies. Posing as a federal, military, or private-sector retiree receiving a pension, our undercover investigator solicited information about the companies and their pension advance products directly from the companies.

Though not generalizable to all pension advance companies, this information provided insights into a variety of pension advance transactions. To describe the marketing practices that pension advance companies employ, we reviewed information provided by the 38 companies that we identified as offering pension advances, including the terms and agreements and the structure of the transactions that they marketed publicly. For the 19 case-study companies, we also obtained additional information during our undercover investigative phone calls, follow-up online quote requests for pension advances, or subsequent documentation that the companies provided on the terms of their pension advance offers.

To evaluate how pension advance terms compare with those of other financial products, for the six companies that provided written quotes to our undercover investigator, we conducted an actuarial analysis of the lump-sum pension advance that we were offered to determine how the pension advance products compare with certain other financial products. For purposes of this report, we considered comparable financial "products" to be loans and lump-sum payment options provided directly by pension plans, as each of these products or offerings have characteristics similar to those of pension advances, such as providing a sum of money and effectively charging interest, or providing a sum of money in exchange for pension plan payments.[9]

To evaluate the extent to which there are federal oversight mechanisms in place related to pension advances, we reviewed criteria from relevant laws and regulations and met with federal and state agencies that have oversight over consumer-protection regulations, financial transactions, and marketing and sales-practice regulations such as CFPB, FTC, and the SEC, as well as members from the North American Securities Administrators Association. We also met with federal agencies that have pension oversight roles such as EBSA, Treasury, PBGC, OPM, DOD, and VA. In addition, we met with advocacy organizations associated with the retired population. We used this information to examine the extent to which federal agencies have undertaken actions to monitor or assess pension advance products' relevance to federal laws and regulations, or provide consumer-education outreach, training, or other oversight efforts.

We conducted this performance audit from August 2013 to June 2014 in accordance with generally accepted government auditing standards. Those standards require that we plan and perform the audit to obtain sufficient, appropriate evidence to provide a reasonable basis for our findings and conclusions based on our audit objectives. We believe that the evidence obtained provides a reasonable basis for our findings and conclusions based on our audit objectives. We conducted our related investigative work from September 2013 to June 2014 in accordance with the standards prescribed by the Council of the Inspectors General on Integrity and Efficiency. For a more-detailed description of our scope and methodology, see appendix I.

BACKGROUND

Pension-Based Products

Pension advances and pension investments are products that, while based on or related to pension benefits, are generally distinct from the pensions themselves. A pension advance is an up-front lump sum provided to a consumer in exchange for a certain number and dollar amount of the consumer's future pension payments plus various fees.[10] Pension investments, the related product, provide investors a future income stream when they make an up-front lump-sum investment in one or more pensioners' incomes.

Multiple parties can be involved in pension advance transactions, including consumers and investors. A pension advance transaction is generally initiated by a pensioner who contacts a pension advance company by telephone, or through an online form. The pensioner provides personal information to the company, including proof of pension payments and the monthly amount the pensioner is currently receiving. After the company collects this information, it may provide one or more quotes to the pensioner, which include estimated monthly amounts that the pensioner is to pay and the lump sum the pensioner will receive. The pensioner may need to provide additional information or documentation that the pension advance company uses to further evaluate the pensioner. Companies perform these evaluations, or underwriting functions, either internally or use an external company. If the company approves the pensioner, it will extend an offer and provide a contract to the pensioner. To move funds among the parties, either the pensioner or the pension advance company may set up a bank account or an escrow account in which the pensioner deposits the future monthly payments and from which the pensioner may receive the lump-sum amount.[11] A company may also require that the pensioner maintain a life-insurance policy to cover the outstanding balance in the event the pensioner dies before all payments are made.[12] After the pensioner signs the contract, the pension advance company gives the lump sum to the pensioner after deducting, if applicable, life-insurance premiums or other fees from the lump sum.

Pension advance companies may also be involved in the related pension investment transaction. These companies can identify financing sources (investors) to provide the lump-sum monies to a specific pensioner or to multiple pensioners. The investor pays the lump-sum amount by depositing the funds into the bank or escrow account that was previously established, as discussed above. The investor receives periodic payments, such as on a monthly basis, over the agreed-upon period either from the pension advance company or through the escrow account. See figure 1 for an illustration of the parties that we identified in the multistep pension advance processes that we reviewed.

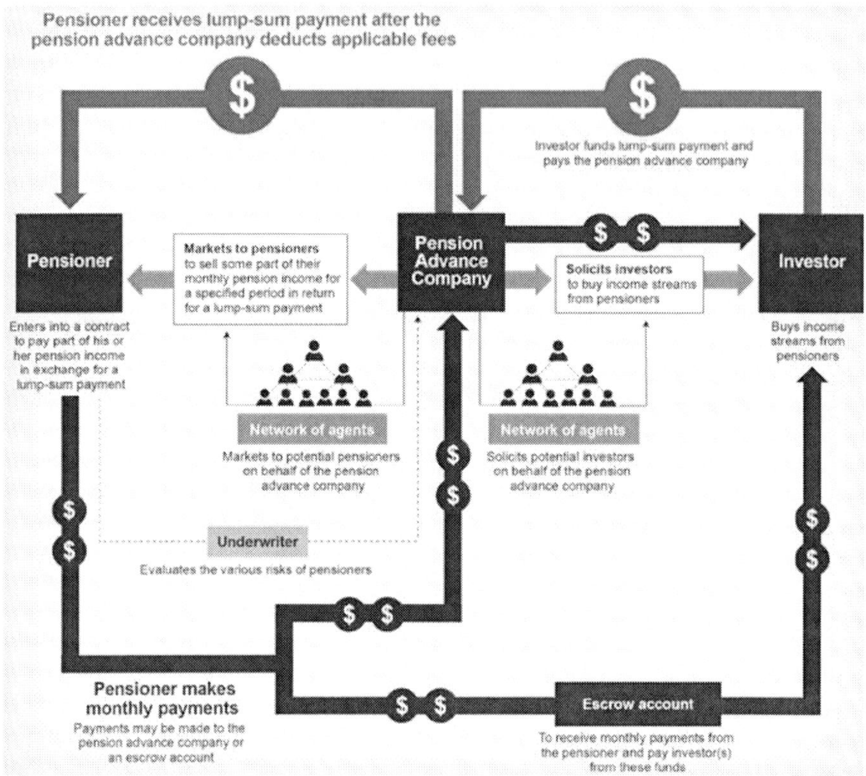

Source: GAO.

Figure 1. Parties Involved in the Multistep Pension Advance Processes That GAO Reviewed.

Federal Laws, Regulations, and Oversight Roles and Responsibilities

Various federal laws could potentially apply to pension advances, depending on the structure of the product and transaction, among other things. For example, certain provisions that prohibit the assignment of benefits could apply to pension advances, depending on whether these advances involve directly transferring all or part of the pension benefit to a third party.[13] Applicable federal laws regarding the assignment of pension benefits include the Employee Retirement Income Security Act of 1974 (ERISA); Title 26 of the United States Code (Internal Revenue Code) governing the tax treatment of retirement and disability plans and payments; Title 5 of the United States Code governing Civil Service Retirement funds; Title 37 of the United States Code governing military members' retirement pay; Title 38 of the United States Code governing certain military veterans' disability pay; and the Railroad Retirement Act of 1974.[14] Depending on the structure of the pension advance product and transaction, other applicable laws could include the Truth in Lending Act (TILA), federal securities laws such as the Securities Act of 1933 (1933 Act) and the Securities Exchange Act of 1934 (1934 Act), provisions on financial education in the Dodd-Frank Wall Street Reform and Consumer Protection Act of 2010 (Dodd-Frank Act), and prohibitions on unfair or deceptive acts or practices contained in the Federal Trade Commission Act (FTC Act) and the Dodd-Frank Act.[15]

Various federal agencies have oversight roles and responsibilities related to consumer and investor issues. CFPB, FTC, and the SEC may have consumer and investor-related oversight roles related to pension advance transactions depending on a number of factors, including the structure of the pension advance product and transaction.

As previously noted, pension advance transactions typically have two sides of the transaction: (1) pension advances and (2) pension investments. CFPB or FTC could have oversight roles over the transactions, depending on the structure of the pension advance product and transaction.[16] The SEC and the Financial Industry Regulatory Authority (FINRA) could have oversight roles over pension advance transactions if the transactions are in connection with the purchase or sale of a security, or if the transaction is recommended by an investment adviser.[17]

Regardless of whether certain pension advance products fall outside the scope of pension antiassignment provisions or TILA, the products themselves or the way in which the products are marketed, offered, and sold could be unfair, deceptive, or abusive.[18] The Dodd-Frank Act gives CFPB broad oversight authority over consumer financial products and services, as well as enforcement and rulemaking authority to prevent unfair, deceptive, and abusive practices in connection with such products and services, and authority to take actions against violators and to educate consumers about ways to protect themselves against such practices.[19] Similarly, FTC has authority to investigate and prosecute unfair or deceptive acts or practices under Section 5 of the FTC Act.[20] Additional details about the Dodd-Frank Act and FTC Act are provided later in this report.

Many other federal agencies may have pension oversight roles related to the pension itself depending on whether the pensioner was a private-sector or federal employee or a military veteran: EBSA, Treasury, and PBGC have oversight over private-sector pensions; OPM has oversight of federal civilian pensions; DOD has oversight over military pensions; and VA has oversight over a needs-based benefit program called a “pension.”[21] The oversight authority that agencies have includes communicating with retirees about matters that affect their pensions.

State Laws, Regulations, and Enforcement

Certain state laws and regulations could also potentially apply to pension advances depending on the way they are marketed, offered, and sold.

For example, potentially applicable state laws include each state’s consumer protection laws such as those governing Unfair and Deceptive Acts and Practices (UDAP) and usury laws that specify the maximum legal interest rate that can be charged on a loan.[22] At the state level, every state has a consumer protection law known as a UDAP law that prohibits unfair and deceptive practices in order to protect consumers, among other relevant state laws. Depending on the overall structure of the products involved, state securities laws could also apply.[23] State securities regulators administer state securities laws and regulations.[24]

During our review, we also identified relevant state investigations and legal cases. For example, in 2013, the states of New York and Massachusetts launched investigations to examine pension advance companies.[25] According to the regulators from these states, these investigations were still under way as of April 2014. In addition to these states’ investigations, there have also been lawsuits filed on behalf of military pensioners and veterans against pension advance companies and affiliates. These lawsuits include class action cases in

California and Georgia. Further, the Arkansas Securities Department has conducted an investigation that resulted in the Commissioner issuing two Cease and Desist Orders against a pension advance company in April 2013 and March 2014.

A NUMBER OF GEOGRAPHICALLY CONCENTRATED AND AFFILIATED COMPANIES ARE INVOLVED IN PENSION ADVANCES AND MARKET TO FINANCIALLY VULNERABLE CONSUMERS NATIONWIDE

The pension advance transactions we reviewed involved a number of geographically concentrated and affiliated companies in the multistep process that we previously described (see fig. 1 for an illustration of the parties that we identified in the multistep pension advance processes that we reviewed). We found that the majority of the 38 companies we identified were affiliated with each other in ways that were not apparent to consumers. Also, the companies that we identified operated primarily as web-based companies, and most marketed to consumers in need of cash or with poor or bad credit nationwide.

About Half of Pension Advance Companies We Identified Were Geographically Concentrated in One State and Offered a Range of Financial Products

We identified at least 38 companies that offered lump-sum advance products in exchange for pension payment streams.[26] (App. II provides summary information on the 38 companies that we identified.) Eighteen of the 38 companies we identified were concentrated in one state, California, and 17 offered a range of financial products in addition to pension advances. See figure 2 for the physical locations of companies that we identified.[27]

In terms of the products and services that these companies offered, we found that 17 out of 38 companies did not exclusively offer pension advances, but also offered lump-sum cash advances for a wide range of income streams, including lottery winnings, insurance settlements, and inheritances. Another 17 companies exclusively focused on offering pension advances.[28]

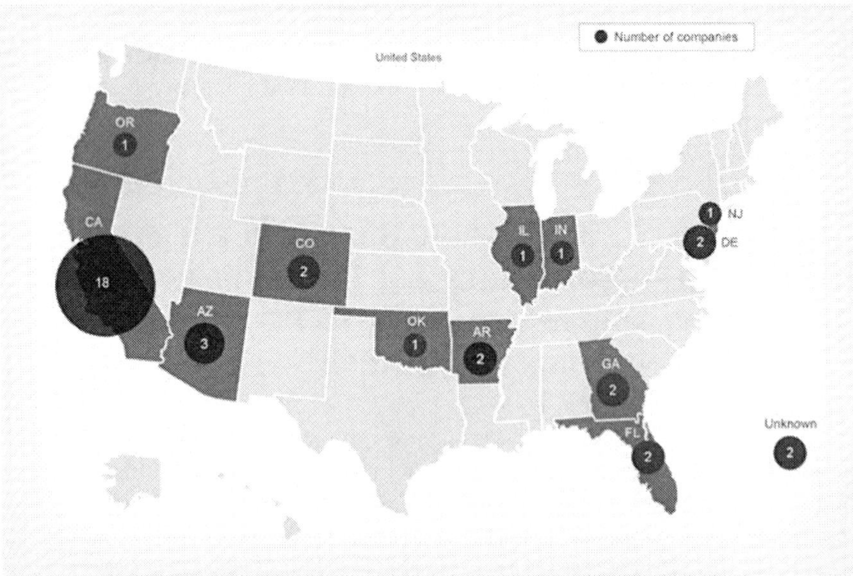

Source: GAO analysis of pension advance company demographics.

Note: The 38 companies that we identified and reviewed either currently or have recently offered pension advance products within the last 2 years.

Figure 2. Locations of 38 Pension Advance Companies Identified by GAO.

Companies We Identified Were Affiliated with Each Other in Various Ways That Are Not Apparent to Consumers

We found that at least 30 out of 38 companies that we identified had a relationship or affiliation with each other, including working as a subsidiary or broker, or the companies were the same entity operating with more than one name.[29] However, only 9 out of those 30 companies clearly disclosed these relationships to consumers on the companies' websites. While companies having affiliations is not uncommon, the lack of transparency to consumers regarding with whom they are actually conducting business can make it difficult to know whom to file a complaint against if the pensioner is dissatisfied or make it difficult to research the reputability of the company before continuing to pursue the business relationship. In some instances, we found that affiliation disclosures occur after a consumer contacts a pension advance company and are not disclosed in marketing materials provided on company websites.

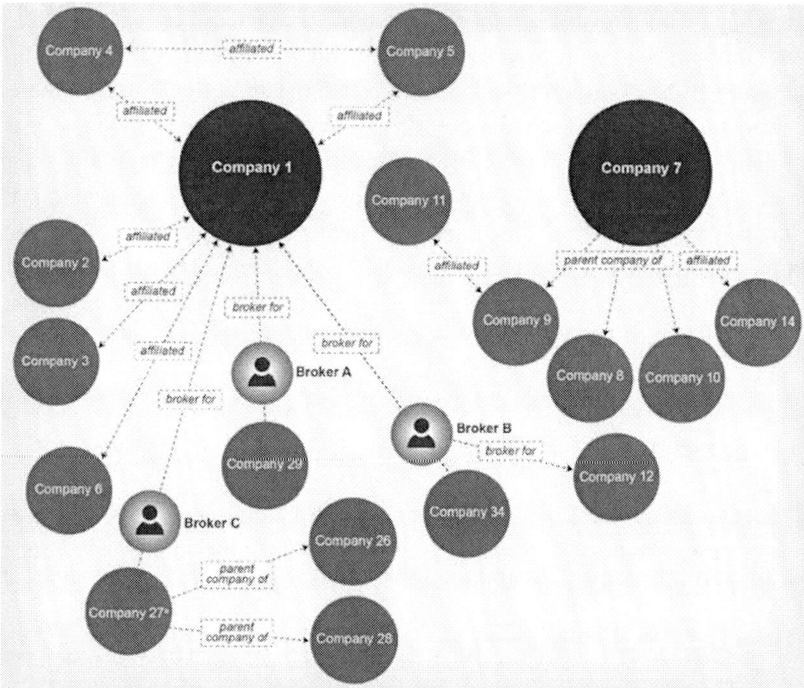

Source: GAO analysis of company information.

Notes: We use the term "affiliated" to refer to companies that have a business relationship. In the figure above, we identify the specific type of affiliation between companies where it was possible for us to clearly document the specific nature of the affiliation from our audit research and investigative work. In some instances, we identified a business relationship, but the nature of the affiliation was unclear. Also, on the basis of our analysis of pension advance companies, there were other related companies. However, the specific relationships between these other companies are unclear and therefore are not presented in the figure above.

[a]This company was formerly known by a different name.

Figure 3. Two Examples of Identified Relationships between Companies Offering Pension Advances.

For example, we were able to identify relationships between 14 companies through our undercover investigative calls, online quote requests, and related e-mail responses from the companies. Similarly, in one complaint filed with FTC, a consumer complained about the lack of disclosure of these affiliations. Specifically, the consumer expressed concerns that the undisclosed relationships between nine pension advance companies on their websites were misleading. This consumer reported that he contacted Company 1 and two other companies that he determined were affiliated with Company 1. It is unclear from the complaint whether the consumer directly contacted the other six companies that he claimed were affiliated. The consumer indicated that his complaint arose after his application was turned down by Company 1 and he was told by another company that if Company 1 denied his application, there would be "no chance" at the other companies because they were owned by Company 1. It is also important to note that complaints may not be accurate or they may not represent a law violation. See figure 3 for an illustration of some of the relationships between companies that we identified.

As highlighted in figure 3, during our audit and undercover investigative work we found evidence that several companies were operating as subsidiaries of a larger company.

- For example, Company 8, Company 9, and Company 10, operated as subsidiaries of Company 7. We were not able to identify a current online presence for Company 7. However, as part of our undercover investigative phone calls, we contacted Company 8, Company 9, and Company 10 and received an e-mail from one of these companies signed by Company 7. Also, during our call with one of those three companies, the representative stated that Company 7 is its parent company. In addition, on their websites, Company 8, Company 9, and Company 10 list the same mailing address. As highlighted in the examples in figure 3, Company 7 is one of the two primary entities we identified as offering pension advance products to consumers.

On the basis of our undercover investigative phone calls and online quote requests to pension advance companies, we identified four instances of companies that operated as brokers for other companies.

- In one instance, we separately contacted both Company 27 and Company 34, and in both instances received a quote by either e-mail or mail from Company 1. These companies did not publicly disclose having a relationship to each other, and maintained separate online presences. However, in the quote documentation we obtained from Company 1, representatives from Company 27 and Company 34 were specifically named as its brokers.

- In another instance, after submitting an online quote request to Company 29, we received a response from that company that contained the logo for Company 1.
- In a third instance, which is not depicted in figure 3, we received e-mails from a representative of Company 17 in response to online quote requests separately submitted to various other companies, including Company 19, Company 20, and Company 25. Also, after submitting an online quote request to Company 21, we received a response that the representative from Company 17 would contact us with a quote.
- In a fourth instance, a separate company representative that we spoke with told us that, although there are many companies with websites, most pension advances are ultimately provided through just a few companies. His comments indicate that many companies could constitute a network of brokers for a few larger companies. (See the sidebar for the direct quote from this representative.) We also heard similar comments from another company representative that we spoke with during our undercover investigative phone calls.

A company representative describing pension advance company affiliations

Company Representative: "As you go to ... their web sites ... they're all going to be the same company pretty much. There's only a couple of companies that do this."

GAO Undercover Investigator: "Oh, okay. Okay. Because I saw a lot of different names."

Company Representative: "Right ... probably 80 percent of all the pensions that get sold in this country ... are through us. There's a couple other companies out there."

Source: GAO investigative call to a pension advance company.

We also identified one company that changed the corporate name that it operated under following legal actions. This company began operating around 1996. In 2005, a class-action lawsuit was filed against that company and its principals for damage restitution, unjust enrichment, and declaratory and injunctive relief. In 2011, the court decided that the plaintiff and class were entitled to restitution in the sum of almost $3 million.[30] Around the time that company filed for bankruptcy in 2012, Company 1 was created under the presidency of one of the executives. As highlighted in figure 3, the company continues to offer pension advances under the name of Company 1 and its affiliates and brokers.

Companies Marketed Products Nationally to Consumers in Need of Quick Cash or with Poor or Bad Credit

At least 34 out of 38 pension advance companies that we identified marketed and offered their services to customers nationwide, operating primarily as web-based companies and marketing through websites and other social-media outlets.[31] Although almost half of the 38 companies that we identified were located in California, we found that most of the 38 companies offered services nationwide. Specifically, the company marketing materials we reviewed did not require customers to come to the company's establishment to complete the pension advance transaction or reside in the same state from which the company was offering services. None of the companies that we spoke with during our undercover investigative calls required that we reside in the location in which they were incorporated or established to conduct business. Twenty-eight of the 38 companies that we identified used marketing materials or sales pitches designed to target consumers in need of cash to address an urgent need such as paying off credit card debts, tuition costs, or medicals bills, or appealed to consumers' desire to have quick access to the cash value of the pension that they have earned. For example, during a phone call with Company 9, the representative marketed her company by stating that her company is the easiest and the quickest to deal with. This theme was also marketed through the companies' websites. Additionally, Company 15 marketed its pension advance product specifically to retirees with federally backed pensions and PBGC-backed pensions, claiming that the pensioner would receive cash quickly. (See the sidebar for an example of one company's marketing on its website.)

Eleven of the 38 companies that we identified used marketing materials or sales pitches designed to target consumers with poor or bad credit. These 11 companies encouraged those with poor credit to apply, stating that poor or bad credit was not a disqualifying factor. Some of these companies specifically stated on their website that pensioners "with poor credit, judgments, past bankruptcies, or other blemishes" are encouraged to apply. We also observed this type of marketing during our undercover investigative phone calls. For example, a representative from one company stated that the company uses a credit report to determine the maximum lump sum that it can provide to the pensioner, and the company will provide several options, stating that no application would likely be declined. In another example, a representative from Company 30 noted that people who call regarding obtaining a pension advance generally have what is considered bad credit, with scores in the 400s and 500s. This representative pointed out that pensioners typically are interested in pension advances because of a financial need. (See the sidebar for the direct quote from this representative.)

Marketing claims featured on a company's website.

"Nowhere else can you leverage your federal or PBGC-backed retirement income by exchanging a future trickle of income for cold, hard cash in your hands today. You've worked hard to earn your money, shouldn't you have control over it?"

Source: A pension advance company.
Note: PBGC is the Pension Benefit Guaranty Corporation.

A company representative describing the credit scores and needs of typical potential customers

"Most of the people that call, they ... have in 4- and 500 score ... which typically it's because they are struggling and they need this money."

Source: GAO investigative call to a pension advance company.

During our undercover investigative phone calls, we observed that 2 of the 19 companies were transparent about the less than favorable terms that the companies offered. For example, one company representative told our undercover investigator that it would be "better" to go to a bank, but advised us that if we could not go through a bank, his company was an option. Another company told our undercover investigator that we would be paying back much less if we went through a bank, but if we did not have any other option then this pension advance would be a way to secure upfront cash. (See the sidebar for the direct quotes from these representatives.)

Two company representatives describing how pension advances compare with bank loans

"[I]f you could go to the bank and do it, you would do better off, but if you can't this is an option."

"[I]f you have access to, like, a bank loan or being able to borrow money from a source that you would be paying back much less ... I always recommend that first, because this is your retirement money that you're using. It can be comparable to, like, a high interest credit card. If you don't have any other options or you don't need the monthly income and you're just wanting to use it for this reason, then of course we want to help you any way we can."

Source: GAO investigative calls to select pension advance companies.

We found that 24 out of 38 companies marketed products to retirees for a range of pensions, including private-sector, military, or government pensions.[32] For example, accepted pensions for the companies we reviewed typically included private, corporate, federal, city, state, teacher, union, military, VA disability, and others. Two companies especially targeted military pensions in that the titles of the companies included either the terms "veterans" or "retired military" and their websites showed a uniform and displayed an American flag. Also, one of these websites included an online shop where one could purchase patriotic merchandise. The other 22 companies did not especially target any particular pension type in their marketing materials. Ten of the 38 companies specifically stated on their websites that they accepted VA disability pensions. However, there were some exceptions noted for the types of pensions that a pension advance company would accept. During our undercover investigative phone calls to 19 companies, one company told us it did not accept government pensions. On pension advance companies' websites, 19 of the 38 companies stated that they did not accept Social Security income, 9 companies stated that they did not accept VA disability benefits, and 1 company specifically stated that it could not accept military pensions. We also found that 5 out of 38 companies marketed to individuals or companies to invest in pension advance funding, at times, through questionable means. For example, two of these companies compared the return on their investment products with other investment products, such as immediate annuities, certificates of deposit, and bonds. In an outgoing voicemail that we heard during our undercover investigative phone calls, one company specifically stated it offered three safe income strategies that are focused on keeping investors' money safe, advertising that it paid more than bank certificates of deposit, money market accounts, and Treasury securities, without the downside risk and volatility of stocks, bonds, and mutual funds. (See the sidebar for a direct quote from this outgoing voicemail message.) However, an investor bulletin issued by the SEC and FINRA highlighted that there are several complex risks associated with investing in pension advances, which we observed that the companies do not completely describe.[33] The risks described in the SEC and FINRA bulletin included: that pension advances are not likely registered with the SEC, which limits reliable information about the products and ability to resolve disputes if necessary; the potential difficulty reselling the product if needed; and potential legal challenges to the investor's "rights" to the income stream that they purchased; among other things. In addition, officials from the PBGC Office of Inspector General told us that a financial advisor, who they identified as acting as a broker, agent, or middleman for a pension sale, fraudulently stated that these pensions were made available for sale by PBGC. Such claims could lead investors to think that these investments are backed by the federal government or PBGC, which is untrue.[34]

A company representative marketing pension advances to investors

"[W]e offer three safe income strategies that are focused on keeping your money safe, paying more than bank [certificates of deposit], money markets, and Treasuries, and doing so without the downside risk and volatility of stocks, bonds, and mutual funds."

"[T]hese strategies work. During the financial market meltdown of 2008, none of our clients lost money due to market volatility. Their money was safe and secure and their income was steady and reliable."

Source: GAO investigative call to a pension advance company.

THE SIX PENSION ADVANCE COMPANIES THAT PROVIDED GAO QUOTES OFFERED UNFAVORABLE TERMS COMPARED WITH OTHER FINANCIAL PRODUCTS

Pension Advance Terms Were Less Favorable than Comparable Regulated Interest Rates and Lump-Sum Calculations

The terms offered by six pension advance companies that provided our undercover investigator with quotes for pension advances did not compare favorably with other financial products such as loans and lump-sum payment options provided directly through pension plans.[35] We compared 99 offers provided to us by six pension advance companies in response to undercover investigative phone calls and online quote requests with those of other financial products.[36] Specifically, we compared the terms with: (1) relevant state usury rates for loans and (2) lump-sum options offered through defined-benefit pension plans.[37] During these calls, we pretended to be either a federal, private-sector, or military pensioner and, based on our analysis, were offered generally similar terms regardless of the type of employer providing the pension. As discussed below, we found that most of the six pension advance companies' lump-sum offers (1) had effective interest rates that were significantly higher than equivalent regulated interest rates, and (2) were significantly smaller than the lump-sum amounts that would have to be offered in a pension plan that provided an equivalent lump-sum option.

Comparison to Usury Rates

When analyzing the effective interest rate for the pension advance offers that we received, we calculated the cost of each lump-sum quote to the annuitant as an effective interest rate.[38] As highlighted in table 1, we determined that the effective interest rate for 97 out of 99 offers provided to our undercover investigator by six companies ranged from approximately 27 percent to 46 percent.[39] Most of these interest rates were significantly higher than the legal limits set by some states on interest rates assessed for consumer credit, known as usury rates or usury ceilings. For example, in comparison to the usury rate for California of 12 percent, we determined that the quotes for lump-sum payments that we received from three pension advance companies for a resident of California had effective interest rates ranging from approximately 27 percent to 83 percent.[40] The effective interest rates on some of these offers could be even higher than the rates we calculated to the extent some pension advance companies require the pensioner to purchase life insurance, and "collaterally assign" the life-insurance policy to the company, to protect the company in the event of the pensioner's death during the term of the contract. For many of the quotes we received, it was unclear whether the pensioner would be responsible for any life-insurance premium payments.[41] See table 1 for additional examples of usury rate comparisons for states where our fictitious pensioners resided for our case studies.

Table 1. Examples of Usury Rate Comparison for Our Pension Advance Offers

State	Number of companies providing offers to fictitious residents of the state	Total number of offers made to fictitious residents of the state[a]	Usury rate of state (percent)	Effective interest rate of offers from companies (percent) [b]
California	3	27	12%	27–83%[c]
Florida	2	7	18	27–38[d]
Maryland	1	63	24	27–46[e]
Texas	2	2	18	27–90 f

Source: GAO analysis of offers received from select pension advance companies in response to our undercover investigative online quote requests and phone calls.

Notes: GAO made undercover investigative online quote requests and phone calls using fictitious profiles of private-sector, federal, and military pensioners residing in these four states.

[a] Companies provided multiple offers to our fictitious pensioners within a single quote request response. For example, for our fictitious military pensioner residing in California, one company provided 24 different offers, another company provided 2 different offers, and the third company provided 1 offer.

[b] The results of our calculation of the effective interest rate of offers from companies are not generalizable.

[c] In its offers, the first company presented the amount of life insurance that would be needed but it is unclear whether the pensioner would need to pay this amount separately, and therefore it is unclear whether the effective interest rate of the pension advance would be higher than calculated. The second company's lump-sum offers did not deduct an amount for a life-insurance premium, and it is unclear whether the pensioner would need to pay this amount separately. Therefore, it is also unclear whether the effective interest rate of the pension advance would be higher than calculated. On the basis of the offers we received from the third company, no life insurance was required. Therefore, it appears that there would be no additional cost to the pensioner for the pension advance.

[d] In its offers, the first company stated that, at closing, two-thirds of the life-insurance coverage cost would be deducted from the offer. The other one-third of the cost would be paid by the company. On the basis of this information, the effective interest rate of the pension advance would be greater than calculated. The second company's lump-sum offers did not deduct an amount for a life-insurance premium, and it is unclear whether the pensioner would need to pay this amount separately. Therefore, it is unclear whether the effective interest rate would be higher than calculated.

[e] In its offers, the company presented the amount of life insurance that would be needed, but it is unclear whether the pensioner would need to pay the premium amounts separately, and therefore it is unclear whether the effective interest rate would be higher than calculated.

[f] On the basis of the offer we received from the first company, no life insurance was required. Therefore, it appears that there would be no additional cost to the pensioner for the pension advance transaction. In its offer, the second company stated that the investor would request that the pensioner have life insurance to "cover the deal in case of ... untimely passing."

Comparison to Lump-Sum Distributions Offered through Pension Plans

We compared pension advance offers that our undercover investigator received to lump-sum options that can be offered in pension plans, where a lump sum can be elected by plan participants in lieu of monthly pension payments. The amount of such a lump-sum option of a private-sector plan must comply with Employee Retirement Income Security Act of 1974 (ERISA) and Internal Revenue Code requirements that regulate the distribution of the present value of an annuity by defining a minimum benefit amount to be paid as a lump sum if a private-sector pensioner chooses the lump-sum option.[42] We determined the minimum lump-sum amount under ERISA rules for private defined-benefit plan sponsors.[43] On the basis of our analysis of 99 pension advances we were offered by six companies, we determined that the vast majority of the offers we received (97 out of 99) were for between approximately 46 and 55 percent of the minimum lump sum that would be required under ERISA regulations. This means that if these transactions were covered under ERISA regulations, the pensioner would receive about double the lump sum that they were offered by pension advance companies.[44] Again, to the extent pension advance companies require the pensioner to pay for life insurance, the terms of the deal would be even more unfavorable than indicated by these lump sum comparisons. See table 2 for a summary of the pension advance quotes as a percentage of the minimum lump sum that would be required under ERISA. Offers varied depending on number of years and the dollar amount to be paid by the pensioner each month. See appendix I for additional information on the basis for the ERISA calculations.

Table 2. Summary of Pension Advance Quotes as a Percentage of Minimum Lump Sum That Would Be Required under ERISA Regulations

Company	Number of offers	Range of pension advancequote as a percentage ofERISA minimum lump sum
Company 19	87[a]	46–55%[b]
Company 15	4	49–54[c]
Company 1	3[d]	54[e]
Company 27	2[f]	51[e]
Company 34	2[g]	77[h]
Company 6	1	55[i]

Source: GAO analysis of offers received from select pension advance companies in response to our undercover investigative online quote requests and phone calls.

Notes: GAO made undercover investigative online quote requests and phone calls using fictitious profiles of private-sector, federal, and military pensioners.

[a] This company provided 63 offers to a fictitious federal pensioner residing in Maryland and 24 offers to a fictitious military pensioner residing in California.

[b] In its offers, the company presented the amount of life insurance that would be needed, but it is unclear whether the pensioner would need to pay this amount separately, and therefore it is unclear whether the ultimate cost of the pension advance would be higher for the pensioner.

[c] This company provided four offers to a fictitious federal pensioner residing in Florida. In its offers, the company stated that, at closing, two-thirds of the pensioner's life-insurance coverage cost would be deducted from the offer. The other one-third of the cost would be paid by the company. On the basis of this information, the cost of the pension advance to the pensioner would be greater than the offers presented.

[d] This company provided three offers to a fictitious federal pensioner residing in Florida.

[e] The company's lump-sum offers did not deduct an amount for a life-insurance premium, and it is unclear whether the pensioner would need to pay this amount separately. Therefore, it is unclear whether the ultimate cost of the pension advance would be higher for the pensioner.

[f] This company provided two offers to a fictitious military pensioner residing in California.

[g] This company provided one offer to a fictitious military pensioner residing in California and one offer to a fictitious private-sector pensioner residing in Texas.

[h] On the basis of the offers we received, no life insurance is required. Therefore, it appears that there would be no additional cost to the pensioner for the pension advance.

[i] This company provided one offer to a fictitious private-sector pensioner residing in Texas. In its offer, the company stated that the investor would request that the pensioner have life insurance to "cover the deal in case of ... untimely passing."

There Is Limited Federal Oversight of Pension Advances

We identified questionable elements of pension advances, such as the lack of disclosure and certain unfavorable agreement terms; however, pension advances currently have limited federal oversight and consumer education from consumer protection agencies such as CFPB and FTC. Further, a number of federal agencies with oversight over pensions, such as EBSA, Treasury, PBGC, OPM, DOD, and VA, reported limited oversight because they have not identified many related complaints and some were just learning about these products.

Questionable Practices Related to Unregulated Transactions Pose Consumer Risks

We identified questionable practices associated with pension advances that currently have little, if any, oversight. Questionable practices that we identified included: (1) the lack of disclosure of terms and company identity as well as (2) certain unfavorable terms of agreements.

Lack of Disclosure of Terms and Company Identity

Whether certain disclosure laws apply to pension advance products depends partly on whether the product and its terms meet the definition of "credit" as set in the Truth in Lending Act (TILA). Although pension advance transactions may resemble loans because a sum of money is provided to a recipient for which the recipient agrees to return a stream of future payments, some companies explicitly stated that their product was not a loan, which, if legally accurate, could exempt them from regulations that require transparency and disclosure under TILA and usury laws. (See additional discussion concerning inconsistencies among companies on whether pension advance products are considered to be loans on page 31.) The federal TILA requires creditors to provide consumers with certain disclosures when they offer or extend consumer credit transactions so as to help consumers understand the terms of the products.[45] Also, as previously described, most states have usury statutes that set the legal limit on finance charges that may be assessed for certain types of credit.

Whether pension advances are actually loans and should be subject to relevant TILA laws is a long-standing unsettled question. In May 2003, the National Consumer Law Center (NCLC) reviewed pension advance company transactions targeting veterans' benefits and reported that, through these product offerings, pension advance companies attempt to circumvent disclosure laws that exist to help consumers make informed decisions about the cost of credit.[46] According to NCLC, by referring to pension advance transactions as something other than loans (for example, one contract it reviewed explicitly stated that the product was not a loan, while another characterized the transaction as a purchase), NCLC asserts that pension advance companies attempt to circumvent TILA consumer protections. More recently, in its 2012 response to CFPB's request for information regarding elder financial exploitation, NCLC reported similar findings. During our own review, we observed that one pension advance company explicitly stated on its website that "in the U.S. pledging one's future pension benefits as collateral for a loan is not legal ... so funding sources must structure their transactions in a strictly unsecured manor [sic]."

We also found that the costs of pension advances were not always clearly disclosed to the consumer and some companies were inconsistent about whether the product is actually a loan.[47] The questionable disclosure practices we identified included the following:

- Thirty-one out of the 38 companies we identified did not disclose to pensioners an effective interest rate or comparable terms on their websites.[48] For loans, under TILA, companies would be required to disclose an effective interest rate for the transaction.
- We also found that some of the offers provided to us by six pension advance companies were not clearly presented.[49] Specifically, these companies provided a variety of offers based on differing number of years for the term as well as differing amounts of the monthly pension to be paid to the company. For example, one company provided a quote including 63 different offers with varying terms and monthly payment amounts to our fictitious federal pensioner residing in Maryland. We considered this volume of information to be overwhelming while not including very basic disclosures, such as the effective interest rate or an explanation of the additional costs of life insurance.
- The full amount of additional fees was not always transparently disclosed in the written quotes that six pension advance companies

provided to our undercover investigator. For example, some of these quotes required life insurance for the pensioner. This, in effect, is an added fee for a pension advance if the life insurance had to be paid for by the pensioner. This type of fee would likely need to be disclosed if this were a loan under TILA. For example, for four of the eight written quotes that companies provided to our undercover investigator, we determined that the companies did not disclose whether the cost of life insurance was deducted from the lump-sum advance or whether the pensioner would need to pay this amount separately, and therefore it was not clear whether the total cost of the pension advance transaction to the pensioner would be higher than quoted. Also, in one of the eight written quotes provided to our undercover investigator, a pension advance company claimed that life insurance is paid for, at least in part, by the pension advance company. However, it was unclear how any pensioner's fees are included in the transaction.[50]

- We also found that some of the 38 companies we reviewed were not consistent in identifying whether pension advances are loans. For example, while nine companies referred to these products as a loan or "pension loan" on their websites, six of these companies stated elsewhere on their websites that these products are not loans. For example, Company 1 stated several times throughout its website that its transaction is not considered a loan. However, on one of its webpages, the company directly referred to one of its pension advance products as a pension loan. Further, two other pension advance companies even have the word "loan" in their name. In addition, during undercover investigative calls to 19 of the companies, we found examples of companies that were not consistent in identifying whether pension advances are loans. In one example, a representative from Company 31 specifically stated that its pension advance is not a loan. In another example, a representative from Company 11 that we spoke with stated that this product was a high-interest loan. He also stated that, for one of the companies he worked with, the pensioner would pay anywhere from 13 to 20 percent interest. In addition, the company's website characterizes the product as a loan in several places. In a third example, a representative from Company 30 did not clearly disclose to our undercover investigator whether or not its pension advance was a loan, when asked. (See the sidebar for the direct quotes from these representatives.)

Company representatives provided differing responses regarding whether a pension advance is a loan

Example 1

Representative from Company 31: "It is not a loan to you ... in the purest sense of an American loan it is not."

GAO Undercover Investigator: "Okay. What is it?"

Company Representative: "It is an advance ... it is treated differently legally."

Example 2

Representative from Company 11:

"Oh it is going to cost you. It really does. It— you are going to pay anywhere on the first company—it is outrageous because see they don't take any collateral, they don't collateralize your pension. They just trust you that you are going to pay it out. What they do is they take an [automated clearing house] and once a month your money comes out of your checking account to them. So it is a high-interest loan. There is no question about it. If you go with the first company it is very high. If you go with the second company you will pay anywhere from 13 to 20 percent interest."

Example 3

GAO Undercover Investigator: "I'm trying to find out ... what you offer... is it a loan ... what is it?"

Representative from Company 30: "Well, it's kind of a—they don't call it a loan. It's—it's a—it's rated as a cash advance ... depending on how you look at it, you can say it's a loan."

Source: GAO investigative calls to select pension advance companies.

As previously discussed, in addition to disclosure of terms, we identified limited disclosure of company affiliations. At least 21 pension advance companies were also affiliated in a number of ways that were not apparent to consumers. These companies may be run by just a few parent companies that operate behind the scenes, which makes it unclear with whom the consumer is dealing. This lack of transparency may also affect a consumer's ability to know whom to contact regarding any problems encountered during the transaction or which regulator to contact to file a complaint, if necessary. As previously described, on the basis of our undercover investigative phone calls and online quote requests to 19 pension advance companies, we identified instances where the company that a consumer contacts may be acting on behalf of another company that provides the pension advance service, or may be operating under multiple names. Regulators from four states that we spoke with that had knowledge of or experience with pension advance products have also observed that these companies are set up in an elusive way, deliberately designed so it is unclear who is involved.

Certain Unfavorable Terms of Agreements

The terms and agreements of pension advances that we reviewed could be unfavorable to consumers, given high effective interest rates. As previously discussed, we calculated that the lump-sum amounts offered by the six pension advance companies to our undercover investigator had effective interest rates that were at times close to two to three times higher than the comparable usury rates legally allowed in the states that these consumers resided in, and that these rates were not clearly disclosed to consumers. NCLC reported, as a result of its review of transactions targeting veterans' benefits, that pension advance companies may be violating state UDAP laws prohibiting fraudulent, unfair, or deceptive practices in the marketplace.[51] In addition, as a result of a class-action lawsuit, a state court also found the characteristics that we identified in pension advances to be unfair. For example, in a class-action suit in California, one of the plaintiffs would have had an imputed interest rate of between approximately 27 and 31 percent. While it found that the agreements at issue in that case are not loans, the court decided that the mischaracterized agreements in the transaction were "unlawful" and "unfair" under California's Unfair Competition Law. The court also found the practice to be "unscrupulous and substantially injurious to consumers."[52] In this case and another lawsuit, pensioners cited that, as a result of these usurious or unfair practices, they paid excess interest to the pension advance companies. Paying excess interest is one type of elder financial exploitation, among others. According to CFPB, elders who lose their life savings as a result of financial elder abuse usually have little or no opportunity to regain what they have lost. Another concern is that, in at least one instance, it appeared that the consumer is limited in his or her ability to challenge the legality of the pension advance agreement. For example, one contract that was submitted as an exhibit of a class-action lawsuit that we reviewed contained language requiring the participant to agree not to raise a claim or defense based on antiassignment laws.

As previously mentioned, there are federal laws and regulations in place to protect consumers from unfair, abusive, or deceptive acts that may be applicable to the questionable practices that we identified. For example, as previously described, the Dodd-Frank Act and the FTC Act contain various provisions prohibiting unfair, abusive, or deceptive acts or practices. Some of the characteristics of pension advance products and their marketing raise questions as to whether they violate these prohibitions. However, there has been no direct federal oversight or public enforcement actions to determine whether pension advance practices violate any of these prohibitions.

Limited Federal Oversight and Consumer Education Related to Pension Advances

Oversight

There is limited federal oversight related to pension advances, which may be in part because, depending on how the product is structured, different federal agencies may have jurisdiction over that particular product.[53] The Dodd-Frank Act gives CFPB broad oversight authority over consumer financial products and services, including enforcement authority to prevent a covered person or service provider from committing or engaging in an unfair, deceptive, or abusive act or practice under federal law in connection with any transaction with a consumer for a consumer financial product or service, or the offering of a consumer financial product or service. The act authorizes CFPB both to take actions against violators and to educate consumers about ways to protect themselves against such practices.[54] In addition, in July 2011, the Dodd-Frank Act also transferred responsibility for implementing TILA, and its consumer protection disclosure requirements, to CFPB. FTC also has authority to enforce TILA and to investigate and prosecute unfair or deceptive acts under Section 5 of the FTC Act.[55] Both the Dodd-Frank Act and FTC Act describe actions that CFPB and FTC are authorized to take to protect consumers and the types of financial and commercial practices that consumers should be protected against, some of which appear to be relevant to practices that we describe in this report. However, neither agency has undertaken any direct oversight or public enforcement actions regarding pension advances. According to CFPB officials, they have provided oversight only in situations where financial products met certain characteristics. According to FTC officials, the agency has not taken any public law-enforcement action and has not received many complaints regarding this issue.

According to CFPB officials, they are concerned about the effect of pension advances on consumers, but stated that they have not taken an official position or issued any regulations regarding pension advance transactions or products, or taken any related enforcement actions. CFPB officials reported that the Assistant Director of its Office of Servicemember Affairs has received a few complaints directly from individual military pensioners, but they are unable to determine if there are more complaints about pension advances because their complaint database does not allow consumers to specifically submit complaints about this type of product.[56] In responding to a draft of our report, CFPB asserted that it has authority over these types of consumer-protection issues and is studying the structure of certain pension advance products and whether activities related to the offering of certain financial products violated any federal consumer financial law within CFPB's authority.

FTC administers the Consumer Sentinel Network, which houses millions of consumer complaints pertaining to a wide range of industries and practices.[57] At our request, FTC officials provided complaint data from the Consumer Sentinel Network about either a list of entities that we initially identified as being involved in pension advances, or complaints containing specific search parameters such as "pension advance" and "pension sale." Through our analysis of these data, we identified 25 complaints related to companies that we determined were involved in pension advances.[58] According to FTC officials, the agency was aware of a few complaints prior to our request, and the number of complaints received is one of several factors used when determining whether to conduct an investigation. It has not undertaken any public law-enforcement actions pertaining to pension advances and noted that it was unable to discuss whether any law-enforcement actions were under way. However, FTC officials reiterated that they identified very few consumer complaints and noted that FTC is governed by a public-interest provision, rather than an obligation to investigate each and every complaint it receives. It therefore focuses its limited resources on matters that tend to affect large numbers of consumers.

By conducting a review to identify whether some questionable practices—such as the ones described in this report—are unfair or deceptive or are actually loans that should be subject to disclosure rules under TILA, and taking oversight or enforcement action if necessary, CFPB and FTC could help ensure that vulnerable pensioners are not harmed by companies trying to exploit them.

As previously mentioned, federal laws prohibiting the assignment of benefits could also be applicable to pension advance transactions, if these transactions involve directly transferring all or part of the benefit to a third party. The transactions that we assessed during our investigative calls did not involve a direct transfer of funds from pension administrators to third parties except for one instance where a company representative acknowledged that this would depend on who is funding the pension. Courts have varied in their interpretation of whether antiassignment laws apply to pension advances, even when they include an indirect transfer of pension benefits.[59]

The securities laws have not been applied to pension advance products. SEC's oversight of companies that issue securities focuses on reviewing the companies' required disclosures rather than examining or supervising the companies. Every offer and sale of a security must be registered with the SEC or exempt from registration under the Securities Act of 1933 (1933 Act).[60] The Securities Exchange Act of 1934 (1934 Act) generally requires brokers or dealers that effect securities transactions, or that induce or attempt to induce the purchase or sale of securities, to register with the SEC.[61] Generally, all registered broker-dealers that deal with the public must become members of FINRA. Member broker-dealers must comply with FINRA rules, which, among other things, require communications used with investors to promote the offer and sale of securities to be fair and balanced, not misleading, and to include certain disclosures regarding the risks and fees associated with the products they offer and sell. Disclosures made under the federal securities laws are also subject to the antifraud provisions of the 1933 Act and 1934 Act, which prohibit material misrepresentations or omissions and provide a general antifraud remedy for purchasers and sellers of securities.[62]

Consumer Education

Consumer financial education can play a key role in helping consumers understand the advantages and disadvantages of financial products, such as pension advances. As we reported in 2013, it can be particularly important for older adults to be informed about potentially risky financial products, given that this population can be especially vulnerable to financial exploitation.[63] The federal government plays a wide-ranging role in promoting financial literacy, with a number of agencies providing financial education initiatives that seek to help consumers understand and choose among financial products and avoid fraudulent and abusive practices.[64] CFPB plays a role in financial education, having been charged by statute to develop and implement initiatives to educate and empower consumers (in general) and specific target groups to make informed financial decisions.[65] The multiagency Financial Literacy and Education Commission, which is chaired by the Secretary of the Treasury and vice-chaired by the director of CFPB, is responsible for coordinating federal financial education efforts.[66]

We found that CFPB and four other agencies had taken actions to provide consumer education on pension advances:[67]

- CFPB's website has a page entitled "Spotlight on Scams That Target Older Adults," added in June 2013, which provides information about the risks of pension advance loans and advice to consumers who are considering them. CFPB also has a short article in the "Ask CFPB" section of its website, added in October 2013, similarly cautioning consumers to be wary of pension advance products, noting product costs can be high. The Federal Deposit Insurance Corporation and CFPB released the training course "Money Smart for Older Adults" in June 2013, which provides information on topics such as common frauds and scams targeting older adults. One of the course's modules covers scams that target veteran benefits and includes information about a pension advance scheme.
- The SEC and FINRA issued a joint Investor Bulletin in May 2013 entitled "Pension or Settlement Income Streams—What You Need to Know Before Buying or Selling Them." The bulletin addresses both pensioners who are considering selling their pensions and investors who are considering acquiring the rights to such pension payments.[68]
- PBGC's fall 2013 newsletter to retirees warned against individuals peddling investments in pension incomes and falsely claiming that PBGC backs them.

However, several other federal agencies—including some that regularly communicate with pensioners as part of their mission—do not provide information about pension advance products and their associated risks and were not aware of CFPB publications at the time of our review.[69] Also, these agencies reported that they have not identified many related complaints and some were just learning about pension advance products. FTC educates consumers on consumer products and avoiding scams through multimedia resources—including its website, print publications, and videos—but it has not provided any specific consumer education about pension advances to date. FTC officials reported that they have not ruled out providing consumer education and the agency is considering taking actions. We also did not identify material on pension advance products in the information or educational material provided by federal agencies in our review that oversee pensions—including EBSA and Treasury, which have oversight over private-sector pensions; OPM, which has oversight of federal civilian pensions; DOD, which has oversight over military pensions; and VA, which has oversight over a needs-based benefit provided to veterans called a "pension."[70] While each of these agencies have existing mechanisms used to inform and educate pensioners (see table 3), only PBGC has used these mechanisms to alert its constituencies to the risks related to pension advance companies.[71] Also, a DOD official told us he contacted CFPB in June 2013 to seek assistance on educational content that might be useful for its pensioners, and CFPB provided this information. However, as of March 2014, DOD had not yet determined how it will use this information.

Table 3. Mechanisms for Federal Agencies to Communicate with Pensioners

Agency	Mechanisms for communicating with pensioners
Employee Benefits Security Administration (EBSA)	EBSA's Office of Outreach, Education, and Assistance fields questions and publishes educational materials and literature to help private-sector pensioners.
Department of the Treasury (Treasury)	Treasury's Internal Revenue Service (IRS) provides educational material on retirementplans to retirees on its website.
Pension Benefit Guaranty Corporation (PBGC)	PBGC publishes a retiree newsletter and makes information available for beneficiaries on its website.
Office of Personnel Management (OPM)	OPM sends benefits administration letters and periodically provides literature as part of outreach efforts after an individual's retirement.
Department of Defense (DOD)	DOD provides education to military members through family centers, which provide family counseling and education. DOD also publishes a retiree newsletter. In addition, DOD officials told us that they could add a warning about pension advance transactions to the bottom of Retiree Account Statements.
Department of Veterans Affairs (VA)	VA provides fact sheets and other educational material to beneficiaries, and posts alerts on its website about matters that may be harmful to beneficiaries.

Source: GAO interviews with federal agencies and review of publicly available educational resources on some of the agencies' websites.

Officials from five of these six agencies agreed that it would be beneficial to use their existing communication methods to inform their respective constituents about pension advances. We have cautioned against overlap—

multiple programs with similar goals and activities—in federal financial education efforts.[72] However, we also have recognized that financial education programs may be more effective if the program's delivery method is adapted so that it is appropriate to its target demographic.[73] Working through the Financial Literacy and Education Commission, CFPB could help ensure that existing consumer-education materials on pension advances are reaching the populations most likely to consider such products by coordinating distribution of such materials with agencies that have oversight over pensions to provide education on the pros and cons and relevant consumer protections associated with pension advances.

CONCLUSION

Some older Americans are both at greater risk of being in financial distress and of being financially exploited as they typically live off incomes below what they earned during their careers and assets that took a lifetime to accumulate. Some pension advance companies market their products as a quick and easy financial option that retirees may turn to when in financial distress from unexpected costly emergencies or when in need of immediate cash for other purposes. However, pension advances may come at a price that may not be well understood by retirees. As illustrated by examples in this report and by related consumer complaints and lawsuits, the lack of transparency and disclosure about the terms and conditions of these transactions, and the questionable practices of some pension advance companies, could limit consumer knowledge in making informed decisions, put retirement funds at risk, and make it more difficult for consumers to file complaints with federal agencies, if needed.

Given the risks associated with pension advance products, the questionable practices that we identified, and the increasing population of retirees, a CFPB review of whether these products violated consumer laws within CFPB's authority could help ensure consumers are not harmed by companies trying to exploit them. Similarly, a formal evaluation by FTC of known information about pension advance companies to determine whether practices such as the ones described in this report are unfair or deceptive, and therefore may warrant related enforcement actions, would contribute to protecting consumers.

While it is important to recognize that even informed people can voluntarily enter into agreements that may not ultimately be in their best long-term financial interests, and therefore bear some responsibility for their choices, awareness of the pros and cons could help in mitigating potential exploitation. More consumer education about the pros and cons associated with pension advances could help consumers understand any associated risks of undertaking these financial transactions, as well as the related consumer protections afforded to them. While CFPB and selected other federal agencies have developed some information and education for consumers on pension advances and the risks they pose, that information is not being disseminated by several federal agencies that regularly communicate with pensioners, in part because the agencies were not aware of these resources. CFPB and the Financial Literacy and Education Commission represent the nexus for interagency coordination on financial education. Working through the commission to coordinate distribution of existing materials on pension advances with the agencies overseeing pensions, CFPB could help ensure that the materials reached the populations most likely to consider such products. Such dissemination also could help increase knowledge about pension advances among federal agency staff interacting with these consumer populations. Finally, these efforts would contribute to a federal financial literacy goal—that consumers have the tools to evaluate whether financial products, such as pension advances, are in their best interests.

Recommendations for Executive Action

In order to strengthen federal oversight or enforcement of pension advance products, we recommend that

- the Director of CFPB review pension advance practices, such as those highlighted in this report, and exercise oversight as appropriate; and
- the Chairwoman of FTC review pension advance companies and the questionable practices that we highlight in this report, and exercise enforcement as appropriate.

To help ensure that consumer-education materials on pension advances reach their target audiences, we recommend that

- the Director of CFPB, through the Financial Literacy and Education Commission, coordinate with the federal agencies that regularly communicate with pensioners—such as EBSA, Treasury, PBGC,

OPM, DOD, and VA—on the dissemination of existing consumer-education materials on pension advances.

AGENCY AND THIRD-PARTY COMMENTS AND OUR EVALUATION

We provided a draft of this report to CFPB and FTC for comment. We also provided relevant sections of a draft of this report to EBSA, Treasury, PBGC, OPM, DOD, VA, the SEC, and FINRA for comment. In addition, we provided selected excerpts of the draft report to NCLC and the North American Securities Administrators Association to obtain their views and verify the accuracy of the information provided.

In its written comments, CFPB concurred with our recommendations that CFPB review pension advance practices and exercise oversight as appropriate and coordinate with the federal agencies that regularly communicate with pensioners on the dissemination of existing consumer-education materials on pension advances. In its response, CFPB stated that it believes that this report provides important insight into potentially questionable activities with respect to pension advance transactions and how they can negatively affect consumers, including older Americans and military veterans. CFPB also stated that it is currently examining potentially improper practices in this area. This action, if implemented effectively and including the practices highlighted in this report, would address the intent of our recommendation. In addition, CFPB stated that it agrees that consumer education must play a key role in helping consumers understand the advantages and disadvantages of financial products, such as pension advances, and that collaboration and coordination among agencies and stakeholders can help educate consumers and prevent future threats to financial stability. In technical comments, CFPB noted that it would not be accurate to say that CFPB has not made a determination about whether it has authority over pension advance products. CFPB clarified that, depending on the structure of a particular pension advance product, CFPB would have authority over certain types of such products and will act on that authority if the offer of a particular product violates applicable federal consumer financial law. In response, we removed language from our recommendation to CFPB that it should make a determination about whether it has authority over these products. Other CFPB technical comments were incorporated into the report, as appropriate.

In an e-mailed response on May 19, 2014, the Director of FTC's Bureau of Consumer Protection agreed with our recommendation and said that she shares GAO's concerns about pension advance products and has directed staff to review this industry and its practices, and, if warranted, to take appropriate law-enforcement action, as we recommended. This action, if implemented effectively, would address the intent of our recommendation. The Director also stated that FTC will coordinate its efforts, where appropriate, with CFPB, pursuant to the memorandum of understanding between the two agencies. In addition, the Director noted that, in determining whether to take enforcement or other action in any particular situation, FTC may consider a number of factors, including the type of violation alleged; the nature and amount of consumer injury at issue and the number of consumers affected; and the likelihood of preventing future unlawful conduct and securing redress or other relief. Further, the Director stated that FTC staff will be accelerating plans to publish consumer-education materials designed to help consumers better understand how these pension advance products work, the advantages and disadvantage of these products, and how consumers can protect themselves when using these products. In technical comments, FTC emphasized that it is primarily a law-enforcement agency with authority over most sectors of the economy and does not have any supervisory authority. In response, we modified the recommendation to FTC to exercise enforcement, as appropriate, rather than oversight. We also clarified in the report that we use the term oversight to include supervisory, regulatory, and enforcement functions. Other FTC technical comments were incorporated into the report, as appropriate.

EBSA, Treasury, PBGC, VA, the SEC, and the North American Securities Administrators Association also provided technical comments that were incorporated into the report, as appropriate. OPM, DOD, FINRA, and NCLC reported that they had no comments.

Stephen M. Lord
Managing Director
Forensic Audits and Investigative Service

Appendix I: Objectives, Scope, and Methodology

This report (1) describes the number and characteristics of entities offering pension advances and the marketing practices that pension advance companies employ; (2) evaluates how pension advance terms compare with those of other financial products; and (3) evaluates the extent to which there are federal oversight mechanisms in place related to pension advances.

To describe the number and characteristics of entities offering pension advances and the marketing practices that pension advance companies employ, we conducted four steps: (1) identifying companies that offered pension advances using public and nonpublic data; (2) obtaining demographic information about these companies; (3) obtaining additional information directly from a subset of companies selected for illustrative example; and (4) reviewing information provided by companies offering pension advances, including the terms and agreements and the structure of the transactions.

1. We identified 38 companies that offered pension advance products by: (1) performing a comprehensive search of companies that market these products to consumers online; (2) conducting queries of public and nonpublic databases that capture information on companies, such as Accurint, the Federal Trade Commission's (FTC) Consumer Sentinel Network, LexisNexis, Dun & Bradstreet, Better Business Bureau, and Proquest databases; (3) conducting library searches of publications that may capture print ads; and (4) interviewing officials from agencies and organizations that provide and collect information to and from retired consumers.[1] We conducted these searches using search criteria such as "pension advances," "pension loans," "pension sales," "cash for pensions," "pension lump sum," "pension buyouts," and "structured settlements."[2] For purposes of this report, we focused more on the pension advance component than on the pension investment component in order to highlight the direct effect on pensioners.

2. For the 38 companies that we identified as having offered pension advance products, we obtained demographic information using public and nonpublic data, including: (1) location, (2) size, (3) annual sales, (4) whether they appear to be affiliated or run by the same owner, (5) range of various types of financial products they offer, and (6) consumer complaints or lawsuits filed against them.[3] To gather demographic data on the entities we identified, we used information provided by the companies on their websites, corroborated and supplemented to the greatest extent possible with public or nonpublic data provided in Accurint, LexisNexis, FTC's Sentinel Network, and any other official databases that we identified with relevant information. On the basis of complaint data that we received from FTC as well as publicly available complaint data, we also identified whether companies had pension advance complaints filed by consumers against them and the nature of such complaints.

3. We obtained additional data on 19 of the 38 pension advance companies selected for case studies, which we use for illustrative examples in this report. To select the case-study companies, we chose companies within 10 selected states[4] based on: (1) varying types of marketing claims or pitches, such as offers, service guarantees, or targeting of specific groups of consumers; (2) presence of or lack of consumer complaints through sources like FTC's database;[5] (3) a range of represented size of businesses;[6] and (4) availability of consumer-friendly information on the company. For these 19 selected companies, we conducted undercover investigative phone calls, submitted online quote requests for pension advances, or obtained documentation directly from the companies. Posing as a federal, military, or private-sector retiree receiving a pension, our undercover investigator solicited information about the companies and their pension advance products directly from the companies. Though not generalizable to all pension advance companies, this information provided insights into pension advance transactions.

4. We reviewed the public marketing strategies employed by the 38 companies, including: (1) what venues they used to market their products; (2) whether any particular group was being targeted; (3) whether companies operated by the same owner were marketing themselves differently; and (4) whether what they included in the advertising clearly disclosed the actual terms they offered. For the 19 case-study companies, we also obtained additional information during undercover investigative phone calls, follow-up online quote requests for pension advances, or subsequent documentation that the companies provided on the terms of these agreements or offers.

To evaluate how pension advance terms compare with those of other financial products, for the six companies that provided written quotes to our undercover investigator, we conducted an actuarial analysis of the lump sum that fictitious pensioners were offered to determine how the pension advance products compare with other financial products. For purposes of this report, we considered comparable financial "products" to be loans and lump-sum payment options provided directly through pension plans, as each of these products or offerings have characteristics similar to pension advances.[7] We assessed the pricing of lump-sum quotes provided by pension advance companies to these two comparable products. In our comparison with loan rates, we calculated the cost of each lump-sum quote to the annuitant as an effective interest rate. The effective interest rate was calculated by equating the lump sum to the amount of a loan, the monthly annuitant payment to a loan repayment amount, and the total number of monthly annuitant payments to the repayment period. We compared the resulting effective interest rate calculations with the usury rate (the legal limit on loan interest rates that can be charged) in the state where the pensioner who received the pension advance offer resided. In our comparison with lump-sum payment options provided directly through pension plans, we determined what the minimum lump-sum amount would be if the lump-sum rules of the Employee Retirement Income Security Act of 1974 (ERISA), which apply to private-sector defined-benefit plans, were applicable to pension advances. We compared the resulting minimum lump-sum calculation under ERISA guidelines with the lump-sum amount offered to our undercover investigator by pension advance companies. To arrive at the ERISA lump-sum amounts, we followed the Internal Revenue Code requirements that determine, for plans that offer lump sums, the minimum amount of such lump sums for the pension plan to remain tax-qualified.[8]

These minimum lump sums vary depending on the form and amount of a participant's promised benefit, the participant's age, and the particular year and month applicable to the calculation, as the interest rates used in the calculation depend on bond market interest rates published by the Department of the Treasury (Treasury), which change from month to month. For this purpose, we used the interest rates applicable to a December 2013 calculation, the most recent rates available at the time of our calculations. In practice, pension plan sponsors that amend their plans to provide onetime offers of lump sums to plan participants (known as lump sum "windows") have some ability to time the applicable month of the calculation, which can sometimes allow sponsors to select a prior month in which interest rates are higher than current interest rates, which lowers the calculated lump-sum amount, to the plan sponsor's benefit.[9] Conversely, sponsors of plans that offer an ongoing lump-sum option do not have this ability, as interest rates in the applicable month of the calculation could be either higher or lower than current interest rates on an ongoing basis. For our calculations, we used interest rates current as of the month of the offer (for almost all of the offers we received, in December 2013) or the month prior to the offer (for a few offers that were obtained in January 2014), so that our hypothetical ERISA lump-sum amounts are most comparable, conceptually, to what pension plans that have an ongoing lump-sum option would offer because we are taking out the intentional variation that a window may have built in.

To evaluate the extent to which there are federal oversight mechanisms in place related to pension advances, we (1) reviewed criteria from relevant laws and regulations regarding pension advances, including those relevant to pension assignments and securities; and (2) identified and assessed federal oversight or consumer-education initiatives related to pension advances.

1. To determine which federal or state laws and regulations are relevant to pension advances, we met with federal and state agencies, and related organizations, that have oversight over consumer-protection regulations, financial transactions, and marketing and sales practice regulations. These entities included Treasury, the Bureau of Consumer Financial Protection (CFPB), FTC, Securities and Exchange Commission (SEC), and the Financial Industry Regulatory Authority (FINRA), as well as the National Association of Attorneys General, North American Securities Administrators Association, and state regulators from Arkansas, California, Florida, and Massachusetts. We also met with federal agencies that have oversight over pensions, such as the Department of Labor's (DOL) Employee Benefits Security Administration (EBSA), Pension Benefit Guaranty Corporation (PBGC), Office of Personnel Management (OPM), Departments of Defense (DOD) and Veterans Affairs (VA), and Treasury. In addition, we met with advocacy organizations associated with the retired population, such as the Pension Rights Center and the National Consumer Law Center. We also identified important state legal cases and investigations to identify the laws or regulations applied in legal or investigative actions taken against pension advance companies.

2. To identify and describe federal oversight initiatives, we interviewed the aforementioned federal agencies about the extent to which they are aware of pension advances, whether they have undertaken any actions to monitor or assess relevance to federal laws and regulations under their jurisdiction, or provided education outreach, training, or other oversight efforts. As part of this assessment, we identified systems and processes at federal agencies that can collect information about complaints on pension advances, and identified whether or how officials used this information to inform their oversight activities. Finally, we reviewed agency documentation to determine what oversight or consumer-education actions agencies have taken.

We conducted this performance audit from August 2013 to June 2014 in accordance with generally accepted government auditing standards. Those standards require that we plan and perform the audit to obtain sufficient, appropriate evidence to provide a reasonable basis for our findings and conclusions based on our audit objectives. We believe that the evidence obtained provides a reasonable basis for our findings and conclusions based on our audit objectives. We conducted our related investigative work from September 2013 to June 2014 in accordance with the standards prescribed by the Council of the Inspectors General on Integrity and Efficiency.

APPENDIX II: ADDITIONAL DETAILS ON PENSION ADVANCE COMPANIES GAO IDENTIFIED

Company number	Location	Life insurance requirement (yes/no)	Affiliated companies identified (company number)	Reference to product as a loan (yes/no)	Part of investigative phone calls[a] (yes/no) (if applicable, type of undercover profile used)	Disposition of phone call	Written quote provided (yes/no)
1	CA	Yes	2 3 4 5 6 27 29 34	Yes[b]	Yes (Federal[c], Private Sector[d], and Military[e])	Company provided a written quote for the federal profile but did not provide one for the private sector or military profiles. The company told the private-sector profile that he did not qualify for the program because he did not have income other than the pension and Social Security. The company failed to send us a quote as agreed for the military profile.	Yes—three offers provided for selling three differing amounts of the monthly pension payment for thefederal profile
2	CA	Unknown	1	Unknown	No	n/a	n/a
3	CA	Unknown	1	No	No	n/a	n/a
4	CA	Unknown	1 5	Unknown	No	n/a	n/a
5	CA	Unknown	1 4	Yes[b]	No	n/a	n/a

Company number	Location	Life insurance requirement (yes/no)	Affiliated companies identified (company number)	Reference to product as a loan (yes/no)	Part of investigative phone calls[a] (yes/no) (if applicable, type of undercover profile used)	Disposition of phone call	Written quote provided (yes/no)
6	FL	Yes	1 13	No	Yes (Private Sector[d])	Company provided [a] written quote.	Yes—one offer provided for a portion of the monthly pension payment
7	CA	Unknown	8 9 10 14	Unknown	No	n/a	n/a
8	CA	No	7 9 10	No	Yes (Private Sector[d])	Company unwilling to provide a quote without performing an instant credit check.	n/a
9	CA	No	7 8 10 11	Yes	Yes (Private Sector[d])	Company unwilling to provide a quote without performing an instant credit check.	n/a
10	CA	No	7 8 9	No	Yes (Military[e])	Company unwilling to provide a quote without performing an instant credit check.	n/a

Appendix II. (Continued)

Company number	Location	Life insurance requirement (yes/no)	Affiliated companies identified (company number)	Reference to product as a loan (yes/no)	Part of investigative phone calls[a] (yes/no) (if applicable, type of undercover profile used)	Disposition of phone call	Written quote provided (yes/no)
11	GA	Yes	9	Yes[b]	Yes (Federal[c])	Company advised us to complete an online quote request. However, the company's online quote request form was limited to submitting contact information rather than submitting an online quote request.	n/a
12	CA	Unknown	34	No	No	n/a	n/a
13	AR	Unknown	6 15 17 18 19 23 24	Unknown	Yes (Federal[c])	Company claimed to never have worked with pensions. However, this company was named in two Cease and Desist Orders issued by the Arkansas Securities Department for violating provisions of the Arkansas Securities Act. This company's pension advance products are described in these orders.	n/a

Company number	Location	Life insurance requirement (yes/no)	Affiliated companies identified (company number)	Reference to product as a loan (yes/no)	Part of investigative phone calls[a] (yes/no) (if applicable, type of undercover profile used)	Disposition of phone call	Written quote provided (yes/no)
14	Unknown	Unknown	7	Unknown	No	n/a	n/a
15	CA	Yes	13	No	Yes (Federalcand Private Sector[d])	Company provided a written quote for the federal profile. The company told the private-sector profile that he would not be eligible for a pension advance because of his income, his age, and the cost of life insurance.	Yes—four offers provided for differing amounts of themonthly pension payment and differing number of years for the terms for the federal profile
16	IL	Yes	17	No	No	n/a	n/a
17	CA	Yes	13 16 18 19 20 21 22 25	No	No	n/a	n/a
18	CA	Yes	13 17	No	No	n/a	n/a

Appendix II. (Continued)

Company number	Location	Life insurance requirement (yes/no)	Affiliated companies identified (company number)	Reference to product as a loan (yes/no)	Part of investigative phone calls[a] (yes/no) (if applicable, type of undercover profile used)	Disposition of phone call	Written quote provided (yes/no)
19	CA	Yes	13 17 20	No	Yes (Federalcand Military[e])	Company provided written quotes in response to the investigative phone call with the military profile as well as a separate online quote request submitted by the federal profile.	Yes—87 offers provided[f]
20	AZ	Yes	17 19 21 22	Yes	Yes (Federal[c])	Company advised us to fill out an online quote request. We then received a response stating that the fictitious pensioner had already been provided with a quote by a related company.	n/a
21	AZ	Yes	17 20 22	No	No	n/a	n/a
22	AZ	Yes	17 20 21	No	No	n/a	n/a
23	AR	Yes	13	No	No	n/a	n/a

Company number	Location	Life insurance requirement (yes/no)	Affiliated companies identified (company number)	Reference to product as a loan (yes/no)	Part of investigative phone calls[a] (yes/no) (if applicable, type of undercover profile used)	Disposition of phone call	Written quote provided (yes/no)
24	Unknown	Yes	13	No	No	n/a	n/a
25	GA	Yes	17	No	No	n/a	n/a
26	CA	No	27	Yesb	Yes (Military[c])	We were unable to reach this company by phone. We submitted an online quote request and received a written quote from Company 27.	n/a
27	CA	Unknowng	1 26 28	Unknown	Yes (Private Sector[d])	We were unable to reach this company by phone. We submitted an online quote request to affiliated Company 26, and Company 27 provided a written quote for our military profile.[g]	Yes—two offers provided for selling two differing amounts of the monthly pension payment for the military profile listed under Company 26 above
28	CA	No	27	No	No	n/a	n/a
29	OK	Yes	1	No	Yes (Militarye)	We were unable to reach this company by phone. We submitted an online quote request and received an e-mail from this	n/a

Appendix II. (Continued)

Company number	Location	Life insurance requirement (yes/no)	Affiliated companies identified (company number)	Reference to product as a loan (yes/no)	Part of investigative phone calls[a] (yes/no) (if applicable, type of undercover profile used)	Disposition of phone call	Written quote provided (yes/no)
						company restating the information provided in the written quote with the header of Company 1. The actual quotes were not provided.	
30	FL	Yes	Unknown[h]	No	Yes (Private Sector[d])	Company requested that we send them an e-mail with our profile information. We did so but did not receive a response.	n/a
31	CA	No	Unknown[i]	No	Yes (Military[e])	Company advised us to submit an online quote. However, the company's online quote request form was limited to requesting contact information rather than submitting an online quote request.	n/a

Company number	Location	Life insurance requirement (yes/no)	Affiliated companies identified (company number)	Reference to product as a loan (yes/no)	Part of investigative phone calls[a] (yes/no) (if applicable, type of undercover profile used)	Disposition of phone call	Written quote provided (yes/no)
32	DE	Unknown	Unknown	Yesb	Yes (Federalc)	We were not able to reach this company by phone. We submitted an online quote request and received information on terms and requirements by e-mail but did not receive a written quote.[i]	n/a
33	DE	No	Unknown	No	Yes (Federalcand Private Sectord)	During these calls, the company either claimed to buy pensions but not "government pensions" or to no longer work with pensions.	n/a
34	IN	Yesj	1 12	Yesb	Yes (Private Sectordand Military[e])	We were not able to reach this company by phone for the military profile. We submitted online quote requests for both our private sector and military profiles, and the company provided written quotes.	Yes—two offers provided[k]

Appendix II. (Continued)

Company number	Location	Life insurance requirement (yes/no)	Affiliated companies identified (company number)	Reference to product as a loan (yes/no)	Part of investigative phone calls[a] (yes/no) (if applicable, type of undercover profile used)	Disposition of phone call	Written quote provided (yes/no)
35	NJ	Yes	Unknown	No	Yes (Private Sector[d])	Received voicemail saying company does not purchase pensions. However, we observed from the company's online marketing that this company did appear to offer pension advances but it did not have an online quote request application.	n/a
36	CO	No	Unknown	Yes	No	n/a	n/a
37	CO	Yes	Other[l]	No	No	n/a	n/a
38	OR	Yes	Unknown	No	No	n/a	n/a

Source: GAO analysis of pension advance company information and results of undercover investigative online quote requests and phone calls.

Notes: n/a = not applicable.

[a]We conducted undercover investigative phone calls to 19 pension advance companies using profiles for fictitious retirees receiving federal, military, or private-sector pensions. We also submitted undercover online quote requests as follow-up in some cases.

[b]Six of the 38 companies we reviewed referred to these pension advance products as a loan or "pension loan" on their websites and stated elsewhere on their websites that these products are not loans.

[c]The federal profile used was a 67-year-old male who carried a life-insurance policy and earned a net pension of $2,567 per month. This fictitious federal pensioner was a resident of either Maryland or Florida. Also, we did not make an investigative phone call to Company 19 using the federal profile and instead submitted a separate online quote quest.

[d]The private-sector profile used was 71-year-old male residing in Texas who carried a life-insurance policy and earned a net pension of $733 per month. Also, we did not make an investigative phone call to Company 34 using the private-sector profile and instead submitted a separate online quote quest.

[e]The military profile was a 44-year-old male residing in California who carried a life-insurance policy and earned a net pension of $925 per month.

[f]This company provided 24 offers to a fictitious military pensioner residing in California and 63 offers to a fictitious federal pensioner residing in Maryland. These offers were for differing amounts of the monthly pension payment and differing numbers of years for the term.

[g]This company did not have an online presence during the time of our review but it operated through Company 26 and Company 28. We submitted an online quote request to Company 26 and received a written quote from Company 27 as a broker to Company 1.

[h]During our undercover investigative phone call with this company, the representative indicated that the company has a working relationship with one or more companies but did not provide additional details about these affiliations.

[i]In the e-mail it sent to the fictitious pensioner, this company claimed to have two lenders interested in speaking with the pensioner about a “pension loan,” and outlined basic terms and requirements that the pensioner would need to meet before continuing with the assessment.

[j]This company’s website stated that life insurance was required for pensioners receiving pension advances for terms of a certain number of years, but that the investor providing the funding would pay for the life insurance in total.

[k]This company provided one offer to a fictitious military pensioner residing in California and one offer to a fictitious private-sector pensioner residing in Texas. Both of these offers were for a portion of the monthly pension payments.

[l]During our audit research, we determined that this company acknowledged an affiliation with another company; however, the affiliated company does not appear to offer pension advance products and is therefore not included in on our list.

End Notes

[1] Pension advance transactions have two major components: (1) pension advances—upfront lump-sum payments provided to consumers in exchange for a certain number (and dollar amount) of the consumers' future pension payments plus various fees and (2) pension investments—pension stream payments provided to investors in exchange for providing the lump sums. For purposes of this report, we focused more on the pension advance component of pension advance transactions, rather than on the pension investment component, in order to focus on the direct impact on pensioners.

[2] MetLife Mature Market Institute et al., *The MetLife Study of Elder Financial Abuse: Crimes of Occasion, Desperation, and Predation against America's Elders*, (New York, NY: 2011). This estimate is based on a study of media reports from April to June 2010. Also, see GAO, *Elder Justice: Federal Government Has Taken Some Steps but Could Do More to Combat Elder Financial Exploitation*, GAO-13-626T (Washington, D.C.: May 16, 2013) for examples of forms of elder financial exploitation. Elder financial exploitation is the illegal or improper use of an older adult's funds, property, or assets. Perpetrators may be family members; paid home care workers; financial advisors or legal guardians; or strangers who inundate older adults with mail, telephone, or Internet scams.

[3] Treasury's Internal Revenue Service (IRS) has an oversight role over private-sector pensions. IRS also has certain oversight roles over governmental plans other than antiassignment provisions. The term governmental plan includes any plan that is established and maintained by a state or local government for its employees as well as any plan that is specified under 26 U.S.C. § 414(d).

[4] Because the pension advances described in this report are based on future pension payments of a specified amount, they are limited to defined-benefit pensions. Defined-benefit plans generally maintain a fund to provide a fixed level of monthly retirement income based on a formula specified in the plan. For purposes of this review, we consider pensions to be the defined benefits typically accepted by pension advance companies as a payment stream for providing an up-front lump sum. These defined-benefit streams include those provided to private-sector retirees through employer-sponsored defined-benefit plans, including plans that have been terminated and are being administered by PBGC, as well as those provided to federal retirees through the Civil Service Retirement System and Federal Employee Retirement System, and to military retirees and veterans through DOD retirement pensions. Although VA does not administer the same kind of defined-benefit pension, we also include its needs-based benefit program for veterans and their survivors that is called a "pension" in our definition of pension in this report.

[5] For purposes of this review, we consider pension advance companies to be entities offering pension advances or an up-front lump-sum payment to consumers in exchange for a certain number of (or an amount equivalent to) future pension payments plus various fees. Also, for purposes of this review, the term "pension advance" does not refer to lump-sum payment options offered directly by pension plans.

[6] For the purposes of this report, we are using the terms "pension advance" and "pension investment" to refer to the two types of products that can be marketed in a pension advance transaction. First, there is the pension advance that is marketed in a transaction between the pension advance company and a pensioner to sell a part of his or her pension benefit for a specific period in return for a lump sum. Second, there is the pension investment that is marketed in a transaction between the pension advance company and potential investors to

invest a lump sum of money to receive a stream of income derived from a pensioner for a specific period.

[7] The 38 companies that we identified and reviewed either currently or have recently offered pension advance products within the last 2 years. We describe this group of companies throughout the report. However, our list of pension advance companies may not capture all companies that exist. Some companies may exist that do not market through the Internet or publications that we reviewed or that do not have documented complaints or register with any of the sources to which we have access. However, we believe that our population effectively describes the minimum level of variation or similarities in pension advance companies and transactions. In addition, as we describe later in this report, some companies included in this total are affiliated with each other. Therefore, the number 38 reflects the number of companies that we identified that present themselves to consumers as separate companies.

[8] We were only able to determine the size of 8 out of 38 companies due to limited information on this characteristic in public and nonpublic databases or on the companies' own websites that we reviewed. Of the 19 companies selected for case studies, 4 companies had consumer complaints and 15 companies had no complaints identified on the basis of our preliminary research for case-study selection.

[9] We considered consumer loans and lump-sum payments offered by pension plan sponsors to be comparable products for purposes of this report. In general, a loan can be defined as money advanced to a borrower, to be repaid at a later date, usually with interest. A loan contract specifies the terms and conditions of the repayment, including the finance charge or interest rate. A lump-sum payment may be offered by certain pension plan sponsors in exchange for an ongoing pension payment. We did not determine whether the pension advances were consumer loans for purposes of the usury laws, whether the pensioner could qualify for lower-interest-rate products, or whether the pensioners were eligible for lump-sum payments from pension plan sponsors. We recognize that there are other consumer financial products that may also be comparable, such as credit cards and other consumer credit products. For purposes of this report, we focus on the two financial products that we believe are most comparable.

[10] Pension advance companies' fees could be deducted from the up-front lump sum paid to the pensioner.

[11] A company may ask the pensioner to arrange an automated clearing house transaction with the bank to make the future monthly deposits.

[12] The pensioner can use an existing life-insurance policy or the pension advance company can provide assistance to the pensioner in obtaining a new policy.

[13] Federal laws regarding pension benefits use terms such as assignment, alienation, and allotment. *Black's Law Dictionary* defines "assignment" as the act by which one person transfers to another, or causes to vest in that other, the whole of the right, interest, or property which he has in any realty or personalty, in possession or in action, or any share, interest, or subsidiary estate therein; "alienation" as giving another party a pension or retirement plan benefits; and "allot" to mean to apportion, to distribute, to divide property previously held in common among those entitled, assigning to each his ratable portion, to be held in severalty, or to set apart specific property, a share of a fund, etc., to a distinct party. For purposes of this report, we use the term "assignment" to also refer to the related terms "alienation" and "allotment." Traditionally, the assignment of a pension has been understood to refer to a substitution of the direct recipient of the pension payments.

[14] 29 U.S.C. § 1056(d); 26 U.S.C. § 401(a)(13), which provides that retirement plan benefits generally may not be assigned or alienated, does not apply to any governmental plan (within the meaning of 26 U.S.C. § 414(d)); 5 U.S.C. §§ 8345(h), 8465(b); 5 C.F.R. § 831.1511; 37 U.S.C. § 701; 38 U.S.C. § 5301(a); and 45 U.S.C. § 231m(a). Also, IRS regulations provide a limited exception for arrangements whereby a participant directs the plan to pay benefits to a third party if: (1) it is revocable at any time; and (2) the third party files a written acknowledgement with the plan that it has no enforceable right to any plan benefit payment. 26 C.F.R. § 1.401(a)-13(e).

[15] 15 U.S.C. § 1605 et seq.; 15 U.S.C. § 78a et seq.; 12 U.S.C. § 5493(d); 15 U.S.C. § 41 et seq.;15 U.S.C. § 45; and 12 U.S.C. § 5531.

[16] For purposes of this report, we use the term oversight to include supervisory, regulatory, and enforcement functions.

[17] At the federal level, the U.S. securities markets are subject to a combination of industry self-regulation (with the SEC's oversight) and direct SEC regulation. This regulatory scheme gives self-regulatory organizations, such as FINRA and national securities exchanges, certain responsibilities for oversight of the securities market and broker-dealers under their jurisdiction. FINRA is involved in various aspects of the securities business, including registering and educating industry participants; examining securities firms; writing and enforcing rules; informing and educating the investing public; providing trade reporting and other industry utilities; and administering a dispute-resolution forum for investors and registered firms. The SEC oversees these self-regulatory organizations to ensure that they are carrying out their regulatory responsibilities.

[18] Provisions prohibiting certain acts or practices may apply if an act or practice is considered: unfair (causes or is likely to cause a consumer reasonably unavoidable substantial injury); abusive (takes unreasonable advantage of a consumer's lack of understanding regarding a product's or service's material risks, costs, terms, or conditions); or deceptive (are misleading, including false representations or misleading price claims, among other things).

[19] According to section 1031 of the Dodd-Frank Act, CFPB may take an enforcement action to prevent a covered person or service provider from committing or engaging in an unfair, deceptive, or abusive act or practice under federal law in connection with any transaction with a consumer for a consumer financial product or service, or the offering of a consumer financial product or service. 12 U.S.C. § 5531. CFPB has the authority to enforce rules prescribed under the FTC Act with respect to an unfair or deceptive act or practice to the extent that such rule applied to an entity under CFPB jurisdiction with respect to the offer or sale of a consumer financial product or service. 12 U.S.C. § 5581(b)(5)(B)(ii).

[20] Under the FTC Act, FTC is empowered, among other things, to (1) prevent unfair methods of competition, and unfair or deceptive acts or practices in or affecting commerce; (2) seek equitable relief for conduct injurious to consumers; (3) prescribe trade regulation rules defining with specificity acts or practices that are unfair or deceptive, and establishing requirements designed to prevent such acts or practices; (4) conduct investigations relating to the organization, business, practices, and management of entities engaged in commerce; and (5) make reports and legislative recommendations to Congress. 15 U.S.C. § 45 et. seq. FTC also has the authority to enforce rules prescribed by CFPB with respect to entities subject to FTC jurisdiction. 12 U.S.C. § 5581(b)(5)(C)(ii). Certain entities, including banks, are excluded from FTC jurisdiction. 15 U.S.C. § 45(a).

[21] As previously described, Treasury also has oversight over certain provisions related to state and local government pensions, which we do not discuss in the scope of this report. Also, VA provides tax-free supplemental income, commonly referred to as VA pension, or non-

service-connected pension, to some low-income wartime veterans who meet certain service, income, and net-worth limits set by law—or people who are surviving family members of veterans who meet the criteria.

[22] Most states have usury statutes, which are regulations governing the amount of interest that can be charged on a loan. These laws specifically target the practice of charging excessively high rates on loans by setting caps on the maximum amount of interest that can be levied. These laws are designed to protect consumers.

[23] For state law purposes, whether pension sales products constitute securities depends on the definition of a security under a particular state's securities laws.

[24] Every state has its own securities laws, commonly known as "Blue Sky Laws," that are designed to protect investors against fraudulent sales practices and activities. These laws vary from state to state, but typically require registration of offerings before they can bc sold in a particular state, as well as licensing of brokerage firms, their brokers, and investment adviser representatives.

[25] In May 2013, the New York Department of Financial Services launched an investigation into pension advances and sent subpoenas to 10 companies engaging in pension advances. According to its press release, the department's investigation is targeted at determining whether these companies have engaged in fraud or misconduct; violated state usury laws; engaged in false, misleading, or deceptive advertising about rates and fees; or violated laws prohibiting the harvesting of military pensions. Also in May 2013, the Massachusetts Securities Division opened an investigation into companies that seek to purchase settlement income streams including pensions of military retirees. As part of this investigation, inquiry letters were sent to nine companies seeking information on whether the company does business in Massachusetts; how and by whom it is marketed; whether residents have been contacted; as well as information needed to determine if the future income streams have been securitized.

[26] The 38 companies that we identified and reviewed either currently or have recently offered pension advance products within the last 2 years. These companies were identified during our audit and are not an all-inclusive list of companies offering pension advance products. Also, these are not necessarily companies that are independent of one another. We discuss affiliations between some of these companies later in this report.

[27] For purposes of this report, the company location listed in the graphic is based on: the address provided by the company on its website; Accurint, Dun & Bradstreet, and Better Business Bureau reports, if available; or legal information provided by the company. Although almost half of the 38 companies that we identified were located in California, we found that most of the 38 companies offered services nationwide, which we further describe later in this report.

[28] The remaining four companies currently or recently offered pension advance products, but detailed marketing materials were not available for our review in order for us to determine whether these companies focused on offering pension advances.

[29] For purposes of this report, we use the term "affiliate" to refer to companies that have a business relationship. In our examples, we identify the specific type of affiliation between companies where it was possible for us to clearly document the specific nature of the affiliation from our audit research and investigative work. In some instances, we identified a business relationship, but the nature of the affiliation was unclear. Securities regulations define a subsidiary as an affiliate controlled by a specific person directly or indirectly through one or more intermediaries. 17 C.F.R. § 230.405. A broker is, among other things,

one who acts as an intermediary or as an agent who negotiates contracts of purchase and sale.

[30] The court decision did not direct the company not to engage in pension advances in the future.

[31] Thirty-six of the 38 companies that we identified had websites, 23 of which provided full online applications for lump-sum pension advances and 7 of which requested contact information only; the remaining companies did not request any information. The other two companies did not have an Internet presence at the time of our review. Although most companies did have websites that would allow them to reach pensioners nationwide, during our undercover investigative calls and review of company websites we identified up to five companies that stated that they do not accept clients either from the states of New York, Arkansas, Massachusetts, Iowa, or Missouri.

[32] We were unable to determine whether 10 companies marketed products to retirees for a range of pensions because these companies did not specify what kind of pensions they deal with in the materials that we reviewed. The remaining four companies currently or recently offered pension advance products, but detailed marketing materials were not available for our review in order for us to determine whether these companies marketed products to retirees for a range of pensions.

[33] As discussed later in this report, the SEC and FINRA coordinated together to issue an Investor Bulletin warning consumers about pension or settlement income streams.

[34] In its fall 2013 newsletter to retirees, PBGC reported that its Office of Inspector General warns that individuals are "peddling fraudulent investments in pension incomes supposedly backed by PBGC." The PBGC Office of Inspector General specifically cited one instance in which a financial advisor claimed that PBGC benefit recipients had sold their pension incomes for a lump sum, and that the benefits, still backed by PBGC, were made available for sale by PBGC. In this alert, PBGC Office of Inspector General reported that this financial advisor further claimed the investments had a guaranteed rate of return of more than 6 percent.

[35] The other 13 companies that we contacted during our undercover investigative work did not provide quotes for pension advances.

[36] We received 99 offers from six pension advance companies in response to our undercover investigative phone calls and online quote requests. We compared the terms of all of these offers to those of other financial products.

[37] We did not determine whether pension advance transactions were loans for purposes of state usury rates, whether the pensioner could qualify for lower-interest-rate products, or whether the pensioner would have been eligible for a lump-sum distribution from the pension plan sponsor.

[38] The effective interest rate was calculated by equating the lump sum to the amount of a loan, the monthly annuitant payment to a loan repayment amount, and the total number of monthly annuitant payments to the repayment period.

[39] In addition, one company provided us with two other offers, one with an effective interest rate of about 83 percent and one with a rate of about 90 percent. These offers were made to residents of California and Texas.

[40] The quotes that we received from these three pension advance companies included 27 different offers for varying monthly payment amounts and time frames. Twenty-six of the 27 offers had effective interest rates ranging from approximately 27 percent to 32 percent; the other offer had an effective interest rate of approximately 83 percent.

[41] According to *Black's Law Dictionary*, collateral assignment refers to assigning an asset whose ownership rights are moving only as an additional security for a loan. These rights will revert to the assignor when the loan is repaid.

[42] 26 U.S.C. § 417(e). The statute also prescribes how the plans must determine the present value of future benefits. In lump-sum options offered through pension plans, the lump-sum election is typically in lieu of the plan participant's remaining lifetime of payments. Because the pension advances used for these examples are for a predetermined number of years, our calculations have been adjusted accordingly.

[43] To arrive at the ERISA lump-sum amounts, we followed the Internal Revenue Code, section 417(e), which determines, for pension plans that offer lump sums, the minimum lump-sum amounts that must be provided for the pension plan to remain tax-qualified. These lump sums vary depending on the form and amount of a participant's promised benefit, the participant's age, and the particular year and month applicable to the calculation. See app. I for additional information on our calculations.

[44] Two of the offers were more favorable with an amount of approximately 77 percent of the minimum lump sum that would be required under ERISA.

[45] Whether a pension advance will be subject to TILA's requirements depends on whether it meets the definitions set out in TILA, including "creditor" and whether the credit is provided for a "consumer" purpose. In July 2011, pursuant to the Dodd-Frank Act, rulemaking, supervision, and enforcement authority for consumer protection laws were generally transferred to CFPB. This includes responsibility for implementing TILA.

[46] National Consumer Law Center, *In Harm's Way—At Home: Consumer Scams and the Direct Targeting of America's Military and Veterans*, (Boston, MA: May 2003). NCLC provides legal and technical consulting and assistance on consumer law issues to legal services, government, and private attorneys representing low-income consumers across the country as well as publishes information on consumer credit laws and unfair and deceptive practices. The organization's attorneys have written and advocated on aspects of consumer law affecting elders and low-income people, including pension advance issues. NCLC attorneys have testified before Congress on these topics and have provided comments to federal agencies on the regulations under consumer laws that affect elders.

[47] As previously described, we reviewed information provided by 38 companies that we identified as offering pension advances, including the terms and agreements and the structure of the transactions that they marketed publicly. For 19 of these 38 companies, we also obtained additional information during our undercover investigative phone calls, follow-up online quote requests for pension advances, or subsequent documentation that the companies provided on the terms of their pension advance offers. In addition, six of these pension advance companies provided written quotes to our undercover investigator.

[48] Three companies did disclose to pensioners an effective interest rate or comparable terms on their websites. The remaining four companies currently or recently offered pension advance products, but detailed marketing materials were not available for our review in order for us to determine whether these companies disclosed an effective interest rate or comparable terms.

[49] As previously described, we received 99 offers from six pension advance companies in response to our undercover investigative phone calls and online quote requests.

[50] In one other written quote, the pension advance company disclosed that life insurance must be in place already. For the remaining two written quotes, the pension advance company disclosed that it did not require life insurance.

[51] NCLC, *In Harm's Way—At Home: Consumer Scams and the Direct Targeting of America's Military and Veterans.*

[52] *Henry v. Structured Investments Co., LLC*, No. 05CC00167, Statement of Decision on Phases 2 and 3 of Bifurcated Trial (Cal. Super. Ct., Sept. 7, 2011).

[53] For purposes of this report, we use the term oversight to include supervisory, regulatory, and enforcement functions.

[54] According to section 1031 of the Dodd-Frank Act, CFPB may take enforcement action to prevent a covered person or service provider from committing or engaging in an unfair, deceptive, or abusive act or practice under federal law in connection with any transaction with a consumer for a consumer financial product or service or the offering of a consumer financial product or service. 12 U.S.C. § 5531. CFPB has the authority to enforce rules prescribed under the FTC Act with respect to an unfair or deceptive act or practice to the extent that such rule applied to an entity under CFPB jurisdiction with respect to the offer or sale of a consumer financial product or service. 12 U.S.C. § 5581(b)(5)(B)(ii).

[55] The FTC Act empowers FTC to, among other things, (1) prevent unfair methods of competition, and unfair or deceptive acts or practices in or affecting commerce; (2) seek equitable relief for conduct injurious to consumers; (3) prescribe trade regulation rules defining with specificity acts or practices that are unfair or deceptive, and establishing requirements designed to prevent such acts or practices; and (4) conduct investigations relating to the organization, business, practices, and management of entities engaged in commerce. 15 U.S.C. § 45 et. seq. FTC also has the authority to enforce rules prescribed by CFPB with respect to entities subject to FTC jurisdiction. 12 U.S.C. § 5581(b)(5)(C)(ii). Certain entities, including banks, are excluded from FTC jurisdiction. 15 U.S.C. § 45(a).

[56] According to a CFPB official, CFPB's consumer database has pre-defined categories from which consumers can choose in order to submit complaints. These fields include categories such as bank account, credit card, money transfer, payday and student loan, or vehicle or other consumer loan. There is no category related to pension advances or option to select "other." Therefore, according to this CFPB official, a consumer would not have an option to directly submit a complaint regarding pension advances in CFPB's database.

[57] FTC's Consumer Sentinel Network is an online database, available to law-enforcement agencies, that compiles consumer complaints received by FTC and law-enforcement and other organizations, including other federal and state agencies and nonprofit organizations. According to FTC officials, complaints from CFPB's complaint database are included in the Consumer Sentinel Network, and, like CFPB's database, the Consumer Sentinel Network does not contain a specific category for pension advance complaints.

[58] On the basis of our analysis of these data, we determined that 12 of the 25 complaints related to pension advances. The remaining 13 complaints do not appear to be related to pension advances but were related to the pension advance companies that we identified.

[59] See examples of variations in rulings on whether pension advances violate antiassignment laws in *In re Pierson*, 447 B.R. 840 (Bankr. N.D. Ohio March 25, 2011); *In re Dunlap*, 458 B.R. 301 (Bankr. E.D. Va. Sept. 13, 2011); and *Henry v. Structured Investments Co.*, LLC, No. 05CC00167, Statement of Decision on Phases 2 and 3 of Bifurcated Trial (Cal. Super. Ct., Sept. 7, 2011).

[60] Securities Act of 1933, 48 Stat. 74 (1933) (codified as amended at 15 U.S.C. §§ 77a *et seq.*). The 1933 Act includes an investment contract in the definition of what constitutes a security. 15 U.S.C. § 77b(a)(1). The Supreme Court held that an investment contract is: (1) an investment of money; (2) in a common enterprise; (3) with the expectation of profits derived from the efforts of others. SEC v. W.J. Howey Co., 328 U.S. 293, 298-299 (1946).

[61] Securities Exchange Act of 1934, 48 Stat. 881 (1934) (codified as amended at 15 U.S.C. §§ 78a *et seq.*). The 1934 Act generally defines a "broker" as "any person engaged in the business of effecting transactions in securities for the accounts of others," and a "dealer" as "any person engaged in the business of buying and selling securities for such person's own account through a broker or otherwise." 15 U.S.C. § 78c(a)(4)(A), (a)(5)(A).

[62] 15 U.S.C. §§ 77q, 78j(b).

[63] GAO-13-626T.

[64] GAO, *Financial Literacy: Overlap of Programs Suggests There May Be Opportunities for Consolidation*, GAO-12-588 (Washington, D.C.: July 23, 2012).

[65] 12 U.S.C. § 5493(d).

[66] In 2003, Congress created the multiagency Financial Literacy and Education Commission, the responsibilities of which include developing a national strategy to promote financial literacy and education, coordinating federal efforts, and identifying areas of overlap and duplication. Pub. L. No. 108-159, Title V, 117 Stat. 1952, 2003 (codified at 20 U.S.C. §§ 9701–08).

[67] The four other agencies that had taken actions to provide consumer education on pension advances included three agencies included in our review—SEC, FINRA, and PBGC—as well as the Federal Deposit Insurance Corporation, which was not included in our review.

[68] Securities and Exchange Commission, Office of Investor Education and Advocacy, *Pension or Settlement Income Streams: What You Need to Know Before Buying or Selling Them*, Investor Bulletin (Washington, D.C.: May 2013).

[69] Officials from FTC, EBSA, Treasury, PBGC, OPM, and VA were not aware of CFPB's various consumer-education publications on pension advances at the time of our review.

[70] Pension plans overseen by these agencies are subject to antiassignment provisions described earlier in this report.

[71] In its fall 2013 newsletter to retirees, PBGC reported that its Office of Inspector General warns that individuals are peddling fraudulent investments in pension incomes supposedly backed by PBGC and clarified that PBGC does not sell, or make available for purchase, pensions or pension incomes.

[72] GAO-12-588.

[73] GAO, *Financial Literacy: A Federal Certification Process for Providers Would Pose Challenges*, GAO-11-614 (Washington, D.C.: June 28, 2011).

End Notes for Appendix I

[1] The 38 companies that we identified and reviewed either currently or have recently offered pension advances within the last 2 years. We describe this group of companies throughout the report. Also, the agencies and organizations that we met with are identified later in this appendix.

[2] Our list of pension advance companies may not capture all companies that exist. Some companies may exist that do not market through the Internet or publications that we reviewed or that do not have documented complaints or did not register with any of the sources for which we had access. However, we believe that our population effectively describes the minimum level of variation or similarities in pension advance companies and transactions. In addition, as we describe in this report, some companies included in this total are affiliated with each other. Therefore, the number 38 reflects the number of companies that we identified that present themselves to consumers as separate companies.

[3] For purposes of this report, the company location is based on: the address provided by the company on its website; Accurint, Dun & Bradstreet, and Better Business Bureau reports, if available; or legal information provided by the company. Also, we were only able to determine the size of 8 out of 38 companies due to limited information on this characteristic in public and nonpublic databases or on the companies' own websites that we reviewed.

[4] The following states were selected based on the number of complaints identified in FTC's consumer complaint database, number of pension advance companies that we identified located in the state, number of residents over age 65 (potential pensioners), and our access to existing licenses or templates for creating licenses for the state—Arizona, Arkansas, California, Delaware, Florida, Georgia, Illinois, Indiana, New Jersey, and Oklahoma. For variation in consumer-protection information outside the states where companies were located, we also selected Maryland and Texas for our review of consumer-protection laws. We also considered whether these states had a larger number of military personnel and represented states with varying degrees of stringency regarding consumer-protection laws. We found that California, Florida, and Texas reflected our desired variation related to these additional considerations.

[5] Of the 19 companies selected for case studies, 4 companies had consumer complaints and 15 companies had no complaints identified on the basis of our preliminary research for case-study selection.

[6] This included both small companies (with up to 500 employees and annual sales below $35.5 million) and companies for which we were unable to determine the size. We did not identify any companies that specifically met our definition of large (more than 500 employees and annual sales greater than $35.5 million).

[7] We considered consumer loans and lump-sum payments offered by pension plan sponsors to be comparable products for purposes of this report. In general, a loan can be defined as money advanced to a borrower, to be repaid at a later date, usually with interest. A loan contract specifies the terms and conditions of the repayment, including the finance charge or interest rate. A lump-sum payment may be offered by certain pension plan sponsors in exchange for an ongoing pension payment. We did not determine whether the pension advances were consumer loans for purposes of the usury laws, whether the pensioner could qualify for lower-interest-rate products, or whether the pensioners were eligible for lump-sum payments from pension plan sponsors. We recognize that there are other consumer financial products that may also be comparable, such as credit cards and other consumer credit products. For purposes of this report, we focus on the two financial products that we believe are most comparable.

[8] 26 U.S.C. § 417(e).

[9] We have ongoing work related to these onetime offers to plan participants.

In: Pension Advance Companies
Editor: Cassidy L. Waller
ISBN: 978-1-63463-539-4

Chapter 2

PENSION ADVANCES: NOT SO FAST*

Federal Trade Commission

"Convert tomorrow's pension checks into hard cash today."

If you're looking for a way to generate cash to make ends meet, a pitch like this may pique your interest. But before you sign on the dotted line, it's important to know what you're getting yourself into.

- Questions to Ask
- Alternatives to Pension Advances
- For More Information

Pension advances, also known as pension sales, loans, or buyouts, require you to sign over all or some of your monthly pension checks for a period of time — typically five to 10 years. In return, you get a lump sum payment, less than the pension payments you sign over. So, unlike other types of cash advances or loans, taking out a pension advance means signing over money you need to live on.

Pension advances aren't cheap: The transactions often include fees that can push the effective annual percentage rate (APR), the cost of credit on a

---

* This is an edited, reformatted and augmented version of the following FTC website, http://www.consumer.ftc.gov/articles/0513-pension-advances-not-so-fast (viewed October 2014).

yearly basis, over 100%. In addition, retirees often are required to buy a life insurance policy — with the pension advance company named as the beneficiary — to insure that the repayments continue.

QUESTIONS TO ASK

If you're considering a pension advance loan, get answers to the following questions:

- *Are you eligible?* Depending on the type of pension you have, you may not be able to sign it over. It might be against the law. Check with your pension administrator for details.
- *What are the costs?* Be aware of all costs and fees. Ask for the APR, which is based on several things, including the amount you borrow, the interest rate and credit costs you're being charged, and the length of your contract. This information may not be disclosed in ads or contracts, so it's important to ask and get it in writing. In addition, there may be other costs or fees, including commissions and life insurance.
- *Do you have to buy life insurance?* Some pension advance companies may require you to buy a life insurance policy naming them as beneficiary. If you die before all the payments you assigned have been received, funds will be paid out from the life insurance policy to cover any remaining balance.
- *What are the tax implications?* Getting a large lump sum can put you in a higher tax bracket. Consult with a tax advisor for information and advice.
- *Can you cancel the transaction?* Maybe not. Some pension advance companies might not let you cancel once you've completed the deal. Make sure you ask the company about its cancellation policy, before you sign the contract, so you know what you're getting into.
- *Are there complaints about the company?* Your local consumer protection, state Attorney General, and the Better Business Bureau can tell you whether any complaints have been filed about a company. Just keep in mind that a lack of complaints doesn't mean the business is on the up-and-up. You may want to do an internet search with the name of the company and words like review, scam, or complaint.

Look through several pages of search results. And check out articles about the company in newspapers, magazines, or online, as well.

Alternatives to Pension Advances

Before you decide to take an advance against your pension, weigh your options.

- Consider a small loan from your credit union or a small loan company. Some banks may offer short-term loans for small amounts at competitive rates. A cash advance on a credit card also may be possible, but it may have a higher interest rate than other sources of funds: find out the terms before you decide. In any case, shop first and compare all available offers.
- Shop for the offer with the lowest cost. Compare the APR and the finance charges, which includes loan fees, interest and other costs.
- If you're considering a pension advance because you're having trouble paying your bills, contact your creditors or loan servicer as quickly as possible and ask for more time. Many may be willing to work with consumers whom they believe are acting in good faith. They may offer an extension on your bills; make sure to find out what the charges would be for that service — a late charge, an additional finance charge, or a higher interest rate.
- Contact your local, non-profit consumer credit counseling service if you need help working out a debt repayment plan with creditors or developing a budget. These groups offer credit guidance to consumers in every state for no or low cost.

For More Information

The FTC works to prevent fraudulent, deceptive and unfair business practices in the marketplace and to provide information to help consumers spot, stop and avoid them. You can file a complaint with the FTC online (www.ftc.gov/complaint) or by phone. Call toll-free, 1-877-FTC-HELP (1-877-382-4357); TTY: 1-866-653-4261. Watch *How to File a Complaint* (http://www.consumer.ftc.gov/media/video-0054-how-file-complaint) to learn more. The FTC enters consumer complaints into the Consumer Sentinel Network, a secure online database and investigative tool used by hundreds of civil and criminal law enforcement agencies in the U.S. and abroad.

To learn more about personal finance issues, visit Money & Credit (http://www.consumer.ftc.gov/topics/money-credit). To learn more about pension advances, read *Pension or Settlement Income Streams—What You Need to Know Before Buying or Selling Them*, from the U.S. Securities and Exchange Commission (SEC) and the Financial Industry Regulatory Authority (FINRA).

In: Pension Advance Companies
Editor: Cassidy L. Waller

ISBN: 978-1-63463-539-4

Chapter 3

PENSION OR SETTLEMENT INCOME STREAMS: WHAT YOU NEED TO KNOW BEFORE BUYING OR SELLING THEM*

U.S. Securities and Exchange Commission

WHAT YOU NEED TO KNOW BEFORE BUYING OR SELLING THEM

Do you receive a monthly pension from a former employer? Are you getting regular distributions from a settlement following a personal injury lawsuit? If so, you may be targeted by salespeople offering you a lump sum today to buy the rights to some or all of the payments you would otherwise receive in the future. Retired government employees and retired members of the military are among those being approached with such offers. Typically the lump sum offered will be less—sometimes much less—than the total of the periodic payments you would otherwise receive.

After acquiring the rights to a future income stream (such as a retiree's pension payments), these pension purchasing or structured settlement companies, sometimes called "factoring companies," may turn around and sell these income streams to retail investors, often through a financial advisor,

* This is an edited, reformatted and augmented version of an Investor Bulletin (SEC Pub. No. 143), issued by Securities and Exchange Commission, Office of Investor Education and Advocacy, May 2013.

broker or insurance agent. These products go by various names—pension loans, pension income programs, mirrored pensions, factored structured settlements or secondary-market annuities. They may be pitched to investors with words like "guaranteed" and "safe"—and may tout robust returns that outpace more traditionally conservative investments such as CDs or money market accounts. The advertised returns may sound enticing, but investors should be aware that these investments can be risky and complex.

FINRA and the SEC's Office of Investor Education and Advocacy are issuing this Investor Alert to inform anyone considering selling their rights to an income stream—or investing in someone else's income stream—of the risks involved and to urge investors to proceed with caution.

What Is a Structured Settlement?

A typical structured settlement involves the resolution of a personal injury or workers compensation lawsuit, which often takes the form of "structured" or periodic payments made to the injured party. The periodic payments are commonly funded by an annuity issued by an insurance company, and are often structured to provide a dependable stream of income and a degree of financial security to the injured party.

SELLING YOUR PENSION OR STRUCTURED SETTLEMENT INCOME STREAM

In a typical transaction, the recipient of a pension or structured settlement will sign over the rights to some or all of his or her monthly payments to a factoring company in return for a lump-sum amount. And the lump-sum amount that factoring companies offer will almost always be significantly lower than the present value of that future income stream. (Simply put, present value is the amount of current money needed to obtain the future stream of payments and is based on a periodic rate of return, such as an interest rate).

Most states require factoring companies that purchase structured settlements to disclose this difference. In California, for example, the disclosure must identify the dollar amount of the payments being sold, the present value of those payments based on a federally established interest rate, the amount being paid to the seller, and the interest rate calculated as if the transfer were a loan and not a sale of the payment rights.

Factors to Consider When Selling Your Income Stream

In uncertain financial times, you may find yourself searching for immediate cash to help pay for rising or unanticipated expenses. For example, even though your pension provides steady income, you may not feel it's enough to make ends meet. At first glance, selling your future pension benefits might seem attractive, especially if mortgage, medical or other expenses loom. Under certain circumstances, these transactions may have their benefits.

However, there are several factors to consider before selling away the rights to your pension or structured settlement income. Transaction costs—including brokerage commissions, legal and notary fees, and administrative charges—can be high. You will need to think about how to replace the cash flow your pension or structured settlement income provides, especially if you depend on that income stream to pay monthly or other expenses. Furthermore, be aware that some salespeople can be aggressive or persuasive when trying to get you to sell your income stream and, in some cases, there may be outright fraud.

Before selling away an income stream you currently receive, ask the following questions:

- Is the transaction legal? Federal law may restrict or prohibit retirees from "assigning" their pension to someone else.1 Furthermore, the secondary sale of a structured settlement often must be approved by a court, in keeping with the Uniform Periodic Payment of Judgments Act (UPPJA). Before selling your pension or structured settlement, you may wish to ask your pension administrator what restrictions may apply, review the terms of your settlement or consult an attorney.
- Is the transaction worth the cost? Find the discount rate that the factoring company has applied to your income stream to arrive at the lump-sum amount. This is in essence the interest rate that is used to bring the future dollars you will receive from your pension into today's present value. The larger the discount rate applied to your pension payments, the lower its value in today's dollars. So, if the factoring company is using a high discount rate, you can expect to receive a lower lump sum. Compare this rate to alternatives such as a bank loan or other options that may be less costly. You should also take into account commissions, fees, and other administrative costs.

- What is the reputation of the company offering the lump sum? Check the factoring company's record with the Better Business Bureau, and research the firm on the Internet and with a financial professional. What complaints have been filed against the company? Were complaints resolved to the customers' satisfaction?
- Will the factoring company require life insurance? When you sell your pension, or even a portion of your pension payments, the factoring company may require you to purchase a life insurance policy. They may require you to name the factoring company, or the investor buying the income stream from them, as the beneficiary of the policy. Should you die before all payments you assigned to the factoring company have been received, funds will be paid out from the life insurance policy to cover any remaining balance. Keep in mind that purchasing a life insurance policy will add to your transaction expenses and reduce your payout.
- What are the tax consequences? The lump-sum payment you collect may be taxable. Discuss the tax implications of any transaction you are considering with a tax professional.
- Does the sale fit your longer-term financial goals? While you may feel you need money now, take time to evaluate your financial objectives down the road. It can be helpful to work with a financial professional who will not receive compensation from, or will not otherwise be involved in, the transaction. You may find that there are other alternatives to deal with your immediate needs. Don't necessarily take the first offer that comes your way.

Investing in Pension or Structured Settlement Income-Stream Products

Recent stock market volatility and a low interest-rate environment have caused investors to look for investments with attractive returns. Buying the rights to someone else's pension or structured settlement income stream may look like a good alternative to other options because advertised yields from 5.75 percent to 7.75 percent are common.

In a typical transaction, the investor buys an income stream product from a financial salesperson for a specific amount. In return, he receives a specific monthly income for a set number of years. While the yield in such a transaction may be attractive, investors should be aware of the following:

- These products can be expensive. You may encounter commissions of 7 percent or higher.
- Pension and structured settlement income-stream products may or may not be securities and likely are not registered with the SEC. As such, reliable information about these products may be difficult to find and resolving disputes should an investment go sour may also be difficult.
- These products are illiquid, which means that they could be difficult to sell. In the event you need money and want to sell the product, you might not be able to do so or you may only be able to do so at a loss.
- Your "rights" to the income stream you purchased could face legal challenges. It may not be legal to purchase someone's pension. And it may be difficult to legally force the original owner of a pension or structured settlement to forward or assign their income to a factoring company or investor.

Before You Invest

Given these risks and complexities, ask the following questions before you invest:

- Is the financial professional selling the product registered with a state or federal regulator or with FINRA? Use the resources below to check the registration status of the salesperson.
    - Visit the SEC's Investment Adviser Public Disclosure (IAPD) website.
    - Visit FINRA BrokerCheck or call FINRA toll-free at (800) 289-9999.
    - Contact your state securities regulator.
    - Contact your state's insurance commission by visiting the website of the National Association of Insurance Commissioners or calling toll-free (866) 470-6242.
- How is the salesperson being compensated? Ask the salesperson how he is compensated and how this impacts the purported rate of return.

- Is the salesperson authorized to sell this product? If registered, ask if the salesperson's compliance department has reviewed the product and allows it to be sold.
- What is the reputation of the company selling the product to me? In addition to checking out the person selling the product, check out the factoring company 's record with the Better Business Bureau and research the firm online and with a financial professional.
- What are the tax consequences? Consult with a tax advisor about the possible tax implications of purchasing pension or structured settlement income-stream products.
- What organization is ultimately paying you? Regardless of who is selling you the product, or the original recipient of the income stream, the ultimate source of payment is likely to be a pension fund (if you are purchasing a pension income stream) or an insurance company (if you are purchasing a structured settlement income stream). You will want to check the financial stability of the organization, because if that entity goes bankrupt or becomes insolvent, it may stop paying the income stream. Research an organization's credit rating and company filings.
- Who is sending the check? In some cases, instead of receiving checks directly from the pension fund or insurance company, it has been reported that some pension sales arrangements allow for the pensioner to manually forward his or her checks to the investor. As a result, in addition to the risk the investment may be difficult to sell and the risk that the pension fund or insurance company's financial position may deteriorate, investors are exposed to the risk that the original pension holder may refuse to forward checks to the buyer. You should make sure that the contract spells out who will be responsible for sending you the payments.
- Whether you are thinking about selling a pension or structured settlement, or buying one from someone else, remember that the risks in doing so are substantial and the safety net if things go wrong may not be very strong. Don't shy away from asking probing questions—and shop around. There may be less risky alternatives to help you achieve your financial objectives.

The Securities and Exchange Commission's Office of Investor Education and Advocacy has provided this information as a service to investors. It is neither a legal interpretation nor a statement of SEC policy. If you have questions concerning the meaning or application of a particular law or rule, please consult with an attorney who specializes in securities law.

End Note

[1] The assignability of pension benefits is addressed in the United States Code, including provisions governing military benefits within 38 USC §5301, civil service benefits within 5 USC §8346(a) and private pension benefits within 29 USC §1056(d).

INDEX

A

B

C

R

S

T

U

V

W

Y

FISH, FISHING AND FISHERIES

ACTION PLAN FOR COMBATING ILLEGAL, UNREPORTED, AND UNREGULATED FISHING AND SEAFOOD FRAUD

CALEB JENNINGS
EDITOR

New York

NOTICE TO THE READER

Library of Congress Cataloging-in-Publication Data

ISBN: 978-1-63483-164-2

Published by Nova Science Publishers, Inc. † New York

CONTENTS

PREFACE

On June 17, 2014, the White House released a Presidential Memorandum entitled "Establishing a Comprehensive Framework to Combat Illegal, Unreported, and Unregulated Fishing and Seafood Fraud." Among other actions, the Memorandum established a Presidential Task Force on Combating Illegal, Unreported, and Unregulated Fishing and Seafood Fraud. The Task Force was directed to report to the President "recommendations for the implementation of a comprehensive framework of integrated programs to combat illegal, unreported, and unregulated (IUU) fishing and seafood fraud that emphasizes areas of greatest need." Those recommendations were provided to the President on December 18, 2014. There are 15 recommendations, which are broad in scope and call on agencies to take concrete and specific actions to combat illegal, unreported, and unregulated (IUU) fishing and seafood fraud throughout the seafood supply chain. This plan articulates the aggressive steps that federal agencies will take both domestically and internationally to implement the recommendations the Task Force made in December 2014. The plan identifies actions that will strengthen enforcement, create and expand partnerships with state and local governments, industry, and non-governmental organizations, and create a risk-based traceability program to track seafood from harvest to entry into U.S. commerce. The plan also highlights ways in which the United States will work with our foreign partners to strengthen international governance, enhance cooperation, and build capacity to combat IUU fishing and seafood fraud. This book addresses the recommendations made by the Task Force.

In: Action Plan for Combating Illegal … ISBN: 978-1-63483-164-2
Editor: Caleb Jennings

Chapter 1

PRESIDENTIAL TASK FORCE ON COMBATING IUU FISHING AND SEAFOOD FRAUD: ACTION PLAN FOR IMPLEMENTING THE TASK FORCE RECOMMENDATIONS*

Presidential Task Force on Combating Illegal, Unreported, and Unregulated Fishing and Seafood Fraud

TASK FORCE MEMBERS

Department of Agriculture (USDA)
Department of Commerce (DOC)
National Oceanic and Atmospheric Administration (NOAA)
Department of Defense (DOD)
The Navy
Department of Health and Human Services (HHS)
Food and Drug Administration (FDA)
Department of Homeland Security (DHS)
U.S. Customs and Border Protection (CBP)

* This is an edited, reformatted and augmented version of a document issued March 2015.

U.S. Immigration and Customs Enforcement (ICE)
U.S. Coast Guard (USCG)
Department of the Interior (DOI)
U.S. Fish and Wildlife Service (USFWS)
Department of Justice (DOJ)
Department of State (DOS)
Bureau of Oceans and International Environmental and Scientific Affairs (OES) Executive Office of the President
Council on Environmental Quality (CEQ) National Security Council (NSC)
Office of Management and Budget (OMB) Office of Science and Technology Policy (OSTP) Office of the U.S. Trade Representative (USTR)
Federal Trade Commission (FTC)
U.S. Agency for International Development (USAID)

Acronyms

APEC	Asia-Pacific Economic Cooperation
CBP	U.S. Customs and Border Protection
CCAMLR	Commission for the Conservation of Antarctic Marine Living Resources
CEP	Cooperative Enforcement Program
CEQ	Council on Environmental Quality
CMAA	Customs Mutual Assistance Agreement
CTAC	Commercial Targeting and Analysis Center
DHS	U.S. Department of Homeland Security
DOC	U.S. Department of Commerce
DOD	U.S. Department of Defense
DOI	U.S. Department of the Interior
DOJ	U.S. Department of Justice
DOL	U.S. Department of Labor
DOS	U.S. Department of State
EEZ	Exclusive Economic Zone
FAO	United Nations Food and Agriculture Organization
FDA	Food and Drug Administration
FTA	Free Trade Agreement
FTC	Federal Trade Commission
FY	Fiscal Year
HHS	U.S. Department of Health and Human Services

HIS	Homeland Security Investigations
HTS	Harmonized Tariff Schedule
IATTC	Inter-American Tropical Tuna Commission
ICE	Immigration and Customs Enforcement
ISE	Information Sharing Environment
ITC	U.S. International Trade Commission
IUU	Illegal, unreported, and unregulated
MDA	Maritime Domain Awareness
MSA	Magnuson-Stevens Fishery Conservation and Management Act
NOAA	National Oceanic and Atmospheric Administration
NOC	National Ocean Council
NSC	National Security Council
OES	Bureau of Oceans and International Environmental and Scientific Affairs
OMB	Office of Management and Budget
OSTP	Office of Science and Technology Policy
PKI	Public Key Infrastructure
PSMA	Agreement on Port State Measures to Prevent, Deter, and Eliminate IUU Fishing RFMO Regional Fishery Management Organization
RICO	Racketeer Influenced and Corrupt Organizations Act
TPP	Trans-Pacific Partnership
T-TIP	Transatlantic Trade and Investment Partnership
TTU	Trade Transparency Unit
UNCLOS	United Nations Convention on the Law of the Sea
UNFSA	United Nations Fish Stocks Agreement
USAID	U.S. Agency for International Development
USCG	U.S. Coast Guard
USDA	U.S. Department of Agriculture
USFWS	U.S. Fish and Wildlife Service
USTR	Office of the U.S. Trade Representative
VMS	Vessel Monitoring System
VTR	Vessel Trip Report
WCPFC	Western and Central Pacific Fisheries Commission
WTO	World Trade Organization

INTRODUCTION

On June 17, 2014, the White House released a *Presidential Memorandum* entitled "Establishing a Comprehensive Framework to Combat Illegal, Unreported, and Unregulated Fishing and Seafood Fraud." Among other actions, the Memorandum established a Presidential Task Force on Combating Illegal, Unreported, and Unregulated Fishing and Seafood Fraud (Task Force), co-chaired by the Departments of Commerce and State with 12 other federal agency members. The Task Force was directed to report to the President within 180 days with "recommendations for the implementation of a comprehensive framework of integrated programs to combat IUU fishing and seafood fraud that emphasizes areas of greatest need." Those recommendations were provided to the President through the National Ocean Council and published in the *Federal Register* on December 18, 2014.

The 15 recommendations are broad in scope and call on agencies to take concrete and specific actions to combat illegal, unreported, and unregulated (IUU) fishing and seafood fraud throughout the seafood supply chain. By circumventing conservation and management measures and engaging in fraudulent practices, entities engaging in IUU fishing and seafood fraud undermine the sustainability of U.S. and global fish stocks and negatively impact general ecosystem health. At the same time, IUU and fraudulent seafood products distort legal markets and unfairly compete with the catch and seafood products of law-abiding fishers and seafood industries. The actions to address these issues fall under four general themes: 1) combating IUU fishing and seafood fraud at the international level; 2) strengthening enforcement and enhancing enforcement tools; 3) creating and expanding partnerships with non-federal entities to identify and eliminate seafood fraud and the sale of IUU seafood products in U.S. commerce; and 4) increasing information available on seafood products through additional traceability requirements. Each of these components is inter-related and complementary such that information and action developed under one supports the others. For example, these actions include establishing an integrated program that traces the path of seafood products from harvest or production to entry into U.S. commerce. This traceability program will feed enhanced information streams into improved enforcement targeting of illegal or fraudulent seafood products through newly integrated risk assessment and enforcement strategies. Similarly, the actions include efforts to improve the international governance of seafood harvest and trade that will complement our domestic efforts. Further, federal agencies are called upon to work with Congress to ensure that officials have the range of authorities necessary to identify and keep IUU seafood and fraudulent seafood products out of U.S. commerce.

Tackling the challenge of IUU fishing and seafood fraud and implementing the broad and integrated set of actions necessary for the task requires a cross-government effort. The full scope of agency expertise, capacity, and authorities reflected in the Task Force membership are vital to the success of this effort.[1] Of the Co-Chairs, the National Oceanic and Atmospheric Administration (NOAA) has broad fisheries management authorities domestically and internationally through Regional Fishery Management Organizations (RFMOs) while the Department of State serves as the U.S. government lead to coordinate U.S. foreign policy and negotiate international agreements related to IUU fishing and seafood fraud.

The Task Force includes such diverse members as the Department of Homeland Security (DHS), which has authorities at the border to inspect and seize commodities such as fraudulent or illegally imported seafood, and the U.S. Agency for International Development (USAID), which supports capacity building efforts that support sustainable fisheries management and legal harvests in developing countries. The Food and Drug Administration (FDA) has established Principles for determining acceptable common and market names for seafood offered for sale in the United States, while the Department of Defense (DOD) contributes efforts to combat IUU fishing through the use of maritime domain awareness tools. The Federal Trade Commission (FTC) protects consumers by addressing business practices that are deceptive to consumers and enhancing informed consumer choices, while the Office of the U.S. Trade Representative (USTR) oversees the development of U.S. trade policy, including seeking commitments in U.S. trade agreements to address IUU fishing and fisheries subsidies and help prevent seafood fraud. While the Task Force members have different missions and areas of focus and expertise, they also have complementary authorities and expertise that can be leveraged to more effectively combat IUU fishing and seafood fraud. For this reason, the recommendations also make the crucial call for Task Force agencies to improve coordination and cooperation with one another.

Implementation of the Task Force's recommendations will begin with the integration of programs and data across the federal government, increased federal agency collaboration, and the development and phased implementation of a traceability program for at-risk species. Some recommendations, including those concerning traceability and ways of identifying seafood fraud, may adapt and evolve along with changing trends in IUU fishing and seafood fraud. It will also be important for Task Force agencies to work with international partners, states, and interested stakeholders in order to adapt to such trends and ensure successful implementation of the recommendations. This Action Plan outlines the Task Force's recommendations and provides key initial steps in implementing each recommendation.

SCOPE AND NATURE OF IUU FISHING AND SEAFOOD FRAUD

The Task Force was established to address both IUU fishing and seafood fraud; however, it is critical to understand the distinctions between the two issues and where they may overlap. Notably, neither issue is limited to fish, but refer to all seafood species, including crustaceans and shellfish.

IUU fishing consists of fishing activities that are illegal, unreported, or unregulated. *Illegal* fishing refers to fishing activities conducted in contravention of applicable laws and regulations, including those laws and rules adopted at the regional and international level. *Unreported* fishing refers to those fishing activities that are not reported or are misreported to relevant authorities in contravention of national laws and regulations or reporting procedures of a relevant RFMO. Finally, *unregulated* fishing occurs in areas or for fish stocks for which there are no applicable conservation or management measures and where such fishing activities are conducted in a manner inconsistent with State responsibilities for the conservation of living marine resources under international law. Fishing activities are also unregulated when occurring in an RFMO-managed area and conducted by vessels without nationality, or by those flying a flag of a State or fishing entity that is not party to the RFMO in a manner that is inconsistent with the conservation measures of that RFMO.

Entities that engage in IUU fishing circumvent conservation and management measures, avoid the operational costs associated with sustainable fishing practices, and may derive economic benefit from exceeding harvesting limits. These entities undermine efforts to maintain harvests of managed stocks at sustainable levels and deprive scientists of data needed to develop recommendations on how to sustainably manage fisheries. Those who engage in IUU fishing practices are also unlikely to observe rules designed to protect the marine environment and its resources from the harmful effects of fishing activity. Examples of such rules include restrictions on the harvest of juvenile fish, gear restrictions established to minimize waste and bycatch of non-target species or harm to the ecosystem, catch limits, and prohibitions on fishing in known spawning areas. To avoid detection, IUU fishers often violate certain basic safety requirements, such as keeping navigation lights lit at night, which puts other mariners at risk. Operators of IUU fishing vessels also tend to deny to crew members fundamental rights concerning the terms and conditions of their labor. Other rules that can be flouted by IUU fishers include those associated with food safety and aquatic animal health, potentially putting consumers and fish populations at risk. Added together, these factors contribute to the unfair advantage that IUU fishing has over fishers who follow the rules and operate under the true costs of sustainable fishing practices.

By its very nature, IUU fishing is difficult to quantify. It can occur in capture fisheries both within areas of national jurisdiction and on the high seas and undermines the sustainability of fish stocks and the broader ecosystem. Because more than 2.5 billion people depend upon fish for food and nutrition, IUU fishing practices threaten food security and sustainability and undermine efforts to reduce global hunger and malnutrition, especially in developing countries. IUU fishing also threatens economic security, impacting livelihoods and potentially contributing to international conflict and conflicts between industrial and small-scale fishers.

The Task Force was also directed to address seafood fraud that undermines the economic viability of U.S. and global fisheries, and deceives consumers about their purchasing choices. Seafood fraud includes mislabeling or other forms of deceptive marketing of seafood products with respect to their quality, quantity, origin, or species (i.e., species substitution). Seafood fraud is generally driven by economic motives and can occur at multiple points along the seafood supply chain. Seafood fraud includes practices like visual enhancement, where a product is made to look better in grade and quality than it actually is. For example, treating tuna steaks with carbon monoxide to make the fish stay red while frozen would be fraud if not noted on the label. Mislabeling quantity includes instances where, for example, added water weight is noted instead of the actual weight of the seafood product by declaring glaze weight as the net weight, or the fish is soaked in water or water is pumped through the fish to change the weight.

Seafood fraud and IUU fishing can overlap when there is mislabeling or other forms of deceptive marketing with respect to origin or species. Species substitution is a form of seafood fraud where, for example, a product is labeled and marketed as a different species than it actually is. This often occurs when a lower value species is represented as a higher value species for economic gain, or vice versa when a higher value species is represented as a lower value species to avoid tariffs. However, species substitution can also occur in attempts to conceal IUU fishing activity, such as when a product's species or origin is mislabeled in order to hide that it is a protected species or from a protected area. Additionally, some seafood is fraudulently comingled and mislabeled or otherwise deceptively marketed in the global supply chain as part of processing and distribution. Marine species may be comingled with freshwater species or freshwater species may be substituted for marine species.

The full extent of seafood fraud is difficult to determine, particularly as it often happens at the retail level. Cooperation with state and local authorities on addressing seafood fraud is essential in strengthening links of the supply chain that occur intrastate, or at the local level, and are sometimes outside federal jurisdiction.

INTERNATIONAL FRAMEWORK

The United Nations Convention on the Law of the Sea (UNCLOS) sets out the basic duty of countries to cooperate in the conservation and management of shared fisheries resources. Other global agreements— such as the 1995 Agreement for the Implementation of the Provisions of the United Nations Convention on the Law of the Sea of 10 December 1982 Relating to the Conservation and Management of Straddling Fish Stocks and Highly Migratory Fish Stocks (UN Fish Stocks Agreement), and the 1993 United Nations Food and Agriculture Organization (FAO) Agreement to Promote Compliance with International Conservation and Management Measures by Fishing Vessels on the High Seas—further spell out the rights and obligations of nations to control their vessels fishing on the high seas and ensure they do not undermine agreed conservation and management rules. The recently negotiated Agreement on Port State Measures to Prevent, Deter, and Eliminate IUU Fishing (PSMA), once in force, will build on these global instruments to add the first set of binding minimum standards specifically intended to combat IUU fishing.

Nations cooperate to manage specific fish stocks through the agreements that establish the Regional Fisheries Management Organizations/ Arrangements (RFMOs). Through the RFMOs, the United States works with members and other participants to develop binding international measures to manage shared fisheries resources and to combat IUU fishing. These measures can include requirements for observer coverage, catch reporting, satellite-based vessel monitoring, and joint boarding and inspection schemes. These organizations are increasingly undertaking transparent and comprehensive compliance reviews to shine a light on those members that do not meet these obligations. Despite this, many RFMO members still face significant challenges in fully implementing RFMO measures due to lack of resources and technical capacity.

The United States also takes an active role in negotiating international guidelines and standards through the United Nations General Assembly and the FAO. These include the FAO International Plan of Action to Prevent, Deter, and Eliminate IUU Fishing, international guidelines on flag State responsibility, and standards to support the establishment of a Global Record of fishing vessels. The United States also works through non-fisheries organizations to support efforts to combat IUU fishing. For example, the International Maritime Organization (IMO)—the United Nations specialized agency responsible for improving maritime safety and security—recently amended its ship identification numbering scheme to allow most large fishing vessels to obtain an IMO number, which facilitates the identification and monitoring of vessels over time despite changes in name, ownership, or flag.

The United States also maintains a number of bilateral and multilateral agreements that facilitate cooperation on fisheries enforcement and monitoring among treaty partners and U.S. government agencies. Bilateral agreements addressing transnational crimes including IUU fishing enable the U.S. Coast Guard (USCG) to put foreign shipriders onboard Coast Guard vessels and aircraft, allowing partner nation law enforcement personnel to exercise their authorities in their Exclusive Economic Zones (EEZs) and over their flagged vessels operating on the high seas. Multilateral agreements allow for the sharing of information, data, and personnel for the purposes of cooperative enforcement efforts and support multilateral large-scale operations.

Trade is another arena where the United States' international efforts can help combat IUU fishing and seafood fraud. The United States is currently engaged in negotiations with 11 other countries in the Trans-Pacific Partnership (TPP), which represents a large percentage of the value of global seafood exports. The United States has set high ambitions for the environment provisions in the TPP, including the incorporation of obligations to end harmful fisheries subsidies that contribute to overfishing and to support measures being developed or implemented through relevant RFMOs and other arrangements in the region, such as catch documentation schemes and port State measures.

U.S. FRAMEWORK

The United States is a global leader in sustainable seafood and is committed to preventing illegally harvested or fraudulently marketed fish from entering the global stream of commerce. This Action Plan reinforces our commitments and underscores our position as a world leader in fighting IUU fishing. As a result of sound science, strong management programs, and enforcement controls the United States has successfully reduced domestic overfishing to its lowest level in decades and rebuilt a record number of historically depleted domestic stocks. IUU fishing and seafood fraud undermine these efforts.

The United States' greatest asset in fighting domestic IUU fishing and seafood fraud is the vast amount of data collected across our U.S. fisheries under the Magnuson-Stevens Fishery Conservation and Management Act (MSA), as well as regulations passed through the regional fishery management councils and regulations promulgated by interstate commissions and states agencies. Data collection requirements begin with the permitting of harvesters and dealers, providing the foundational information to cross-reference all other subsequent data collected. Permits are required for almost any person who will sell or purchase fish or fish products harvested from U.S. waters from the vessel, or who will sell such fish. Permitting requirements vary by fishery, but at a minimum they include the permit holder's name and contact information along with vessel identification information (e.g., name and registration/USCG documentation/IMO Number) and authorized activity. These permits establish the framework for data collection for covered species.

The MSA also provides tools for combating IUU fishing conducted by non-U.S. flagged fleets. Among other things, this process focuses on the actions that foreign governments take to ensure that vessels flying their flag do not violate sustainable management measures adopted by various regional fisheries management organizations. Foreign governments that are found to have vessels engaged in such activities may be identified in a biennial report to Congress as having vessels engaged in IUU fishing. Countries may also be identified for having vessels that fish illegally in U.S. waters or for overfishing of stocks shared with the United States (with adverse impacts on such stocks), in areas without applicable international measures or management organizations. NOAA's National Marine Fisheries Service (NOAA Fisheries) will engage in consultations with these newly identified nations to press for corrective action. If sufficient action is not taken, prohibitions on the importation of certain fisheries products into the United States and the denial of port privileges for fishing vessels of that nation may be levied.

While at sea, permitted domestic commercial fishing vessels are often required to have operational Vessel Monitoring Systems (VMS) on board to track their location and movement in the U.S. EEZ and treaty waters. The U.S. VMS program currently monitors more than 4,000 vessels and is the largest national VMS program in the world. Permitted domestic commercial harvesters can also be required to submit a vessel trip report (VTR) for each fishing trip prior to landing. The VTR provides a detailed report of the vessel's fishing activity, including trip duration, location of fishing activity, gear used, catch harvested, catch composition (species and weight for both landed and discarded fish), and identity of who is purchasing the landed catch. This information can be verified by enforcement or by on-board and/or portside monitoring programs where used. At the point of sale, or entry into U.S. commerce, permitted dealers are often required to submit purchase records. These records can include species data that can be cross-referenced with landing records provided by the vessel. These data are collected, managed, and shared on the national, regional, and local level by NOAA Fisheries; the Atlantic Coastal Cooperative Statistical Program and the Pacific Fisheries Information Network, which are cooperative state-federal programs that design and implement marine fisheries statistics data collection and integrate those data into a single data management system; state agencies; and other partners.

As a result of the data collection programs in place for U.S. fleets, domestic fishery activities are of less concern relative to seafood fraud, though problems with species substitutions exist at the retail level in grocery stores and restaurants and could occur when U.S. product is processed overseas. Domestic fish and fishery products harvested under a federal fisheries management plan have low incidences of species substitution. Similarly, state-managed fisheries have a high incidence of compliance, though product traceability is more difficult as a result of information delays and the large number of separate systems in place.

The Food and Drug Administration (FDA), Federal Trade Commission (FTC), and U.S. Department of Agriculture (USDA) all play important roles in preventing seafood fraud, including with respect to species, net weight, Country of Origin Labeling, or any other attributes important to the supply chain and consumers. For example, under the Federal Food, Drug, and Cosmetic Act, all seafood products are subject to examination by FDA authorities at import and must provide information to ensure that they meet the same standards as domestic seafood products—they must be sanitary, wholesome, safe to eat, and contain informative and truthful labeling in English. In addition, NOAA also operates a voluntary, fee-for-service Seafood Inspection Program (SIP) to inspect seafood processing facilities and products at various points in the supply chain for the purpose of label and species verification. In total, the SIP annually inspects approximately 20 percent of domestic consumption annually. Non-compliant products that are discovered can be barred from further entering U.S. commerce or referred to the appropriate enforcement agencies.

Further, NOAA's Office of Law Enforcement (NOAA OLE), Department of Homeland Security (DHS) components (U.S. Coast Guard, U.S. Customs and Border Protection (CBP) and U.S. Immigration and Customs Enforcement (ICE)), the FDA, and the U.S. Fish and Wildlife Service (USFWS) all have complementary authorities to collect information; make inquiries, examinations, inspections, searches, seizures, and arrests to ensure compliance with U.S. laws; and seize or refuse entry of cargo when necessary. Good cooperation exists between the relevant enforcement entities and efforts are being made under this Action Plan to further enhance the interagency cooperation to address the issue of seafood fraud.

CHALLENGES

The United States remains committed to preventing illegally harvested and mislabeled seafood from entering into U.S. commerce, but the complexities of the global seafood supply chain pose a number of challenges to doing so. For example, even with the large network of international agreements and measures available, combating IUU fishing in international waters remains a complex challenge. IUU fishing fleets move easily from fishery to fishery and region to region. Few countries have the resources or capacity to directly monitor the expanses of international waters. While the obligations for the control of vessels are clear under international law, the legal tools to enable nations to control the actions of their nationals are less so. Domestically, several critical statutes lack robust civil judicial and criminal enforcement authority, adequate administrative penalties, or appropriate forfeiture authority to address IUU and fraudulently marketed seafood products. These low and disproportional penalties are often factored in as "the cost of doing business" and pose a serious challenge to deterring illegal actions.

There are particular challenges for law enforcement. Over half of the world's fish production is processed at sea or soon after landing, which in many cases renders the species unidentifiable without forensic laboratory analysis. NOAA, CBP, and FDA have forensic laboratories with the capability to conduct DNA testing of fish in suspected fraud cases, but have not been able to significantly expand efforts to effectively address the issues of seafood fraud and IUU fishing. Further, the information collected for seafood imports is not as comprehensive as that required under domestic fisheries regulations, with limited exceptions for certain high-value species. Once the seafood products have entered U.S. commerce, this less-extensive information limits the ability to distinguish between and track illegally imported seafood products once they flow into the distribution chain, creating significant challenges for maintaining effective chain of custody.

Further, fraud that occurs at the retail (i.e., restaurant and supermarket) level is difficult to address as retail sales are predominantly regulated by the state and local authorities. Effective implementation of initiatives aimed at preventing the trafficking of IUU and fraudulently marketed fish is often made more difficult by the simple fact that there are inconsistent rules across agencies regarding how to properly identify the name and origin of seafood products.

The Task Force's Action Plan to implement its recommendations to the President helps tackle these challenges by leveraging the capabilities and authorities of its federal agency members. For example, by determining concrete steps and timelines to better share critical data in a timelier manner across federal agencies and ensuring consistency in the way agencies identify the name and origin of seafood products, agencies will be able to more effectively deal with the challenges of the seafood supply chain in combating IUU fishing and seafood fraud.

How We Got to This Point

It is in the interest of the United States to promote a comprehensive framework that supports sustainable fishing practices while combating seafood fraud and the sale of IUU seafood products, including by improving the transparency and traceability of the seafood supply chain. To achieve these objectives, the United States must improve and enhance the implementation, application, and coordination of the tools available to combat IUU fishing and seafood fraud to the maximum extent allowed by law. The Task Force was established to identify and achieve these objectives.

After its establishment, the Task Force initiated a public engagement process to gain broad input to inform and advise the development of these recommendations. This process included two public meetings, two webinars, a diplomatic message to countries with fisheries interests and marine coastlines, and a public comment period noticed in the *Federal Register*. The Task Force also analyzed the federal government's existing authorities to combat IUU Fishing/Seafood Fraud Committee, and identified potential gaps in those authorities. It further examined specific areas for improved coordination between the Task Force agencies and broader U.S. government efforts regarding these issues. For example, this Task Force recognizes the importance of coordinating with related efforts under the Presidential Task Force on Wildlife Trafficking, the White House Strategy to Combat Transnational Organized Crime, and the President's Interagency Task Force to Monitor and Combat Trafficking in Persons.

Based on this public engagement process and the Task Force's analysis of existing authorities, gaps in those authorities, and current and potential levels of interagency coordination, the Task Force developed 15 recommendations designed to enhance the tools currently available to combat IUU fishing and seafood fraud. The recommendations were published in the *Federal Register* on December 18, 2014, as well as in a diplomatic message to foreign countries with fisheries interests and marine coastlines, soliciting comment on the implementation process of each recommendation. The Task Force received valuable feedback from domestic stakeholders and international partners on the 15 recommendations and will continue the process of engaging stakeholders and international partners as it implements the recommendations.

The following Action Plan for the 15 Task Force recommendations lays out more detail on the scope of the action in question, how agencies translate the recommendations into action, and—most importantly—a timeline and lead entities for implementation. Oversight of this Action Plan will be carried out by the National Ocean Council (NOC), which will establish a standing IUU Fishing/Seafood Fraud Committee (NOC Committee) to take the place of the Presidential Task Force on Combating IUU Fishing and Seafood Fraud. The NOC Committee will be co-chaired by NOAA and the Department of State, includes all current members of the Task Force, and may incorporate other agencies as required and approved by the NOC.

RECOMMENDATION 1. INTERNATIONAL – PORT STATE MEASURES

Work with Congress to pass implementing legislation for the Port State Measures Agreement (PSMA). Direct the Secretary of State to promote entry into force and full implementation of the PSMA.

Rationale

The absence of binding multilateral port State measures has hindered the process of addressing IUU fishing. With the United States as a driving force, the FAO adopted the Agreement on Port State Measures to Prevent, Deter and Eliminate IUU Fishing (PSMA). The PSMA envisages that Parties, in their capacities as port States, will take a series of steps to ensure that foreign vessels do not land or transship IUU seafood in their ports, thus preventing such seafood products from entering markets. Among other things, the PSMA requires Parties to: designate ports to which foreign vessels may request entry and to require such vessels seeking port entry to provide advance notice with detailed information relevant to their fishing activities and fish on board; inspect an appropriate number of foreign vessels that have entered their ports to determine whether the vessels were engaged in or supported IUU fishing; and cooperate with port States in the implementation of PSMA with respect to their flagged vessels.

The PSMA requires 25 ratifications to enter into force; to date there are 11 with 14 more required. In the United States, the Senate provided advice and consent to join the Agreement in 2014, but ratification is pending the passage of implementing legislation in Congress. U.S. ratification will help ensure consumer confidence in the seafood supply chain by helping keep illegal product out of the market. It will demonstrate strong leadership in the global battle against IUU fishing and encourage broad ratification of the PSMA by other countries. Global implementation of robust port State controls on port access will disrupt IUU fishing vessel operations by decreasing the ports where IUU fishing products can be landed and increasing the costs associated with IUU fishing.

Implementation Steps

Lead agencies: NOAA and the Department of State.

The implementation plan for this recommendation is comprised of two components: a domestic agenda and an international agenda. Specific implementation steps include:

- Continue to work with Congress to support timely adoption of legislation necessary for ratification and effective implementation of the PSMA.
- *By July 2015*, facilitate briefings for key Congressional Committees, Members, Caucuses, and staff with agency leadership and stakeholders, to highlight linkages between the PSMA and efforts to combat IUU fishing, and the benefits of entry in force and robust implementation of the PSMA globally to domestic fishing interests. Keep these efforts going through the remainder of 2015 and beyond as needed.
- Use existing fora such as Capitol Hill Oceans Week in June 2015 to continue to discuss the PSMA and its benefits with Congressional members, staff, and constituents.
- Through direct diplomatic outreach, identify at least 14 countries that are supportive of the PSMA and work with them to ratify the Agreement as soon as possible and ideally *by the end of 2015.* Continue to advocate for speedy entry into force and broad implementation of the Agreement in international fora such as regional fishery management organizations (RFMOs), the United Nations, and FAO's Committee on Fisheries.
- Identify impediments to ratification of the PSMA by foreign partners and provide information and assistance to help overcome those obstacles as feasible and appropriate.
- Continue efforts to support, and provide technical assistance to, developing countries seeking to ratify and implement the PSMA.
- Ensure that the PSMA remains a top priority for senior officials' dialogues with foreign State representatives.

RECOMMENDATION 2. INTERNATIONAL – BEST PRACTICES

Direct the Task Force to develop, within one year (and refine as appropriate in subsequent years), best practices for catch documentation and data tracking; high seas boarding and inspection; monitoring, control, and surveillance measures (including observer programs, vessel tracking systems, authorized vessel lists); port State control; and compliance monitoring and promote their adoption in each of the Regional Fishery Management Organizations (RFMOs) of which the United States is a member.

Rationale

Effective management of internationally shared fish stocks requires cooperation among nations to develop the necessary monitoring, control, and surveillance measures to ensure that all follow the agreed upon rules. Different RFMOs have adopted different measures over the years, and they are often developed ad hoc within each organization and not always updated in light of improvements in technology or other advances. Particularly among the RFMOs that manage similar fish stocks, consistent and up-to-date measures that reflect best practices will facilitate enforcement, eliminate loopholes, and improve cooperation. At the same time, there is no one-size-fits-all solution. Effective use of these tools also means identifying which tools fit best with the specifics of each fishery or region.

Article 21 of the 1995 United Nations Fish Stocks Agreement (UNFSA) establishes a reciprocal high seas boarding and inspection regime that is a critical tool for greater cooperation in enforcement of RFMO-adopted conservation and management measures. This regime serves as the best-practice model for RFMO schemes. To date only the Western and Central Pacific Fisheries Commission (WCPFC) has implemented measures to the full extent outlined in UNFSA, and the United States will continue to seek adoption of comparable regimes in the other RFMOs to which it is a party.

Implementation Steps

Lead Agencies: NOAA and the Department of State Other agencies involved: DOJ.

This work, and particularly efforts to regularly update it into the future, may also be rolled into efforts to revise and further implement the U.S. National Plan of Action to Prevent, Deter, and Eliminate IUU Fishing.

- *By June 2015,* NOAA and the Department of State will convene an interagency group to evaluate existing RFMO measures related to monitoring, control, and surveillance (including port State controls) and compliance monitoring, related U.S. regulations, and input received from U.S. and international comments on the draft recommendations. The interagency group will identify best practices among these existing measures, including evaluating their overall effectiveness and the status of implementation and compliance by RFMO members with the various measures. The work will also include identifying the circumstances in which a particular tool might be most effective or appropriate.
- *By September 2015,* the interagency group will complete a set of best practices, including, as appropriate, model text and/or key elements that could form the basis of RFMO measures.
- *By December 2015,* U.S. delegations to RFMOs will begin, as appropriate given existing measures, to advance proposals to adopt new, or modify existing, measures based on these best practices, including UNFSA-consistent high seas boarding and inspection regimes. Specific proposals will also take into account input from relevant U.S. constituent Advisory Committees appointed to advise the U.S. delegations to each RFMO.
- *By December 2015,* based on the results of expert work convened by the FAO to develop best practices for catch documentation and trade tracking, the interagency group will, as appropriate given existing measures, expand this work to include multilateral catch documentation schemes.

RECOMMENDATION 3. INTERNATIONAL – MARITIME DOMAIN AWARENESS

Direct the Secretaries of Defense and Homeland Security to include IUU fishing threat analysis and monitoring as a component of U.S. and international efforts to increase overall maritime domain awareness.

Rationale

The National Maritime Domain Awareness (MDA) Plan promotes favorable conditions for global maritime security and prosperity through the effective understanding of the maritime domain and by improving our ability to appropriately share information, including intelligence, law enforcement information, and all-source data from the public and private sectors. The Plan promotes improved domain awareness through enterprise-level access to data and encourages broad interaction and expanded collaboration among members of the Global Maritime Community of Interest—an informal community of all levels of domestic and international government along with private and commercial maritime stakeholders, bound by the common interest of maintaining the maritime domain for global security and prosperity.

The U.S. Departments of Homeland Security (DHS), Defense (DOD), and others have contributed to the development of enterprise tools—common services, capabilities, and processes—to increase awareness of the maritime domain. These tools can bring tremendous value when applied to the efforts of the United States and its foreign partners in combating IUU fishing. Many in the U.S. government are unaware of these enterprise tools or lack training on how to apply these tools to conduct IUU fishing threat analysis and monitoring. In addition to the challenges faced within the U.S. government, many foreign governments may lack an appropriate (i.e., unclassified, Non-Public Key Infrastructure (nonPKI), etc.) Information Sharing Environment (ISE)—the people, projects, systems, and agencies that enable responsible information sharing for national security—with the necessary access to maritime data, automated analytics, and information sharing capabilities would enhance their ability to combat IUU fishing. The Task Force believes that improving awareness of enterprise tools within the U.S. government and establishing an appropriate information sharing environment between U.S. and foreign partner users would increase the awareness of decision-makers responsible for combating IUU fishing.

This recommendation does not alter existing constitutional or statutory authorities or responsibilities of agency heads to carry out operational activities or to exchange information. It does however, direct the Secretaries of Defense and Homeland Security to ensure tools and capabilities used to increase overall maritime domain awareness support IUU fishing threat analysis and monitoring.

Implementation Steps

Lead Agencies: DOD and DHS.
Other Agencies Involved: NOAA and the Department of State.

DHS and DOD will assemble a U.S. government interagency team to identify enterprise tools used by the MDA community that could be applied to combating IUU fishing and ensure linkage of those tools to the strategy developed pursuant to Recommendation 8.

- By May 2015 the Department of State, NOAA, and DOD will co-host a workshop to gain better understanding into relevant surveillance and enforcement technologies currently being piloted to support management in marine protected areas around the globe.
- By September 2015 the team will: Catalogue existing initiatives. Establish an Enterprise Tools IUU Fishing Implementation Planning Team.Produce a report on findings to inform an implementation plan.
- By December 2015, the Enterprise Tools IUU Fishing Implementation Planning Team will formulate an implementation plan with timelines to support efforts to enhance IUU fishing threat analysis and monitoring.
- By December 2015, the Secretaries of Homeland Security and Defense will provide a report to the NOC Committee on developing an appropriate environment for sharing information between U.S. and foreign government partner users in order to enhance threat analysis and monitoring, which would increase the awareness of decision-makers responsible for combating IUU fishing.

RECOMMENDATION 4. INTERNATIONAL – FREE TRADE AGREEMENTS

Direct the U.S. Trade Representative to use existing Free Trade Agreements (FTAs) and future FTAs to combat IUU fishing and seafood fraud, including through enhanced cooperation with our trading partners and commitments to enforce environmental and labor laws.

Rationale

U.S. Free Trade Agreements (FTAs) and environmental cooperation programs can help to combat IUU fishing and seafood fraud and support sustainable fisheries management by helping to develop management practices and tools in FTA partner countries. For example, FTAs with Korea, Panama, Colombia, and Peru require these trading partners to "adopt, maintain and implement" laws, regulations, and any other measures to fulfill obligations under a number of relevant multilateral environmental agreements—including those establishing the Commission for the Conservation of Antarctic Marine Living Resources (CCAMLR) and the Inter-American Tropical Tuna Commission (IATTC)—as well as to "adopt and maintain" in its statutes, regulations, and practices fundamental internationally recognized labor rights. U.S. FTAs also contain obligations that require U.S trading partners to "effectively enforce" their environmental and labor laws, including laws that protect and conserve natural resources, such as marine fisheries. These obligations are subject to dispute settlement under the trade agreement, and the Office of the U.S. Trade Representative (USTR) has authority to monitor and review implementation of these and other FTA commitments. Other U.S. agencies provide support for implementation of FTA commitments through technical assistance and labor and environmental cooperation programs. U.S. FTAs also support cooperation to enforce consumer protection laws, achieve compliance with respective laws and regulations on customs matters, and encourage the use of voluntary market mechanisms to protect the environment and natural resources.

The United States, with USTR as the lead agency, is also in the process of negotiating trade agreements with 11 other countries for a Trans-Pacific Partnership (TPP) agreement and with the European Union for a Transatlantic Trade and Investment Partnership (T-TIP) agreement, together representing more than 70 percent of the value of all global seafood imports. In these negotiations, the United States is pursuing commitments to ensure effective enforcement of labor and environmental laws, as well as to address specifically IUU fishing activities, including the implementation of port State measures. The United States will seek similar commitments in future FTAs as well.

Implementation Steps

- *In 2015,* conclude TPP negotiations, including provisions to effectively enforce labor and environmental laws and to combat IUU fishing and seafood fraud, where appropriate. Prepare the agreement for Congressional consideration, seek to put the agreement into force as quickly as possible, and monitor implementation of the agreement.
  Lead Agency: USTR
  Other Agencies Involved: Coordination with relevant agencies, as appropriate, including DHS, FDA, DOJ, and the Departments of State and Commerce.
- *In 2015,* continue to develop proposals with the European Union to effectively enforce labor and environmental laws and to combat IUU fishing and seafood fraud, where appropriate. Seek to conclude T-TIP negotiations with a robust outcome as soon as possible, and thereafter prepare the agreement for Congressional consideration, seek to put the agreement into force, and monitor implementation of the agreement.
  Lead Agency: USTR
  Other Agencies Involved: Coordination with relevant agencies, as appropriate, including DOJ, DHS, and the Departments of State and Commerce.
- Continue to prioritize implementation of FTA commitments to effectively enforce labor and environmental laws, including laws pertaining to the conservation and management of marine fisheries resources, through, inter alia, regular meetings of FTA labor and environment bodies.
  Lead Agencies: USTR, Department of Labor (DOL), and the Department of State
  Other Agencies Involved: Coordination with relevant agencies, as appropriate, including DOJ, DHS, the Departments of State, Commerce, and the Interior (DOI), the Environmental Protection Agency and USAID.

- Develop and enhance labor and environmental cooperation programs, where appropriate, including to support existing and future FTA partner commitments to effectively enforce labor and environmental laws and to address IUU fishing. In coordination with DHS, use FTAs as a vehicle to enhance customs cooperation and information sharing on IUU fishing and the fraudulent importation of fish and seafood.
  Lead Agencies: DOL and Department of State.
  Other Agencies Involved: Coordination with relevant agencies, as appropriate, including DOI, DOJ, the Department of Commerce, the Environmental Protection Agency, USAID, and USTR.

RECOMMENDATION 5. INTERNATIONAL – FISHERY SUBSIDIES

Direct the U.S. Trade Representative, and the Secretaries of State and Commerce to pursue international commitments to eliminate fisheries subsidies that contribute to excess fishing capacity, overfishing, and IUU fishing by 2020.

Rationale

While some fisheries subsidies provide important benefits like supporting fisheries research and conservation, subsidies that contribute to overfishing and overcapacity are one of the main drivers of unsustainable levels of fishing. Such subsidies also undermine the effectiveness of fisheries management regimes and can contribute to IUU fishing. Global fisheries subsidies were estimated at approximately $35 billion in 2009, of which approximately $20 billion consisted of capacity-enhancing subsidies.

The United States has long been a global leader and advocate in support of disciplines on harmful fisheries subsidies, and the United States has long identified disciplines on fisheries subsidies as a key area in which trade agreements can contribute to environmental conservation and sustainable development. Since 2001, as part of the Doha Round of World Trade Organization (WTO) negotiations, the United States has pursued commitments to limit harmful fisheries subsidies and provide greater transparency for fisheries subsidies. The United States will continue to seek and support multilateral commitments in the WTO on fisheries subsidies. In the Asia-Pacific Economic Cooperation (APEC) forum the United States is promoting transparency in fisheries subsidies and their ultimate elimination, as reflected in the 2014 Xiamen Declaration of the APEC Ocean-Related Ministerial Meeting. The United States is also pursuing ambitious commitments to discipline harmful fisheries subsidies in our ongoing free trade agreement negotiations for a Trans-Pacific Partnership (TPP) agreement with 11 other Asia-Pacific countries and a Transatlantic Trade and Investment Partnership (T-TIP) agreement with the European Union.

Implementation Steps

To implement this recommendation, USTR, along with the Departments of State and Commerce and other relevant agencies, will continue to pursue meaningful commitments to discipline harmful fisheries subsidies and promote greater transparency of fisheries subsidies. Specific steps include:

- *In 2015,* conclude negotiations on the TPP environment chapter, including commitments on some of the most harmful fisheries subsidies, such as those linked to IUU fishing, and to enhance transparency and reporting requirements for fisheries subsidies programs. Seek Congressional approval for the TPP agreement and seek to put the agreement into force as quickly as possible.
  Lead Agency: USTR.
  Other Agencies Involved: Coordination with relevant agencies, as appropriate.
- *In 2015,* seek, with the European Union, proposals to discipline harmful fisheries subsidies, and to enhance transparency and reporting requirements for fisheries subsidies in the T-TIP agreement. Seek to conclude negotiations with a robust outcome on fisheries subsidies as soon as possible, and prepare for Congressional consideration and subsequent entry into force of the T-TIP agreement.
  Lead agency: USTR.
  Other Agencies involved: Coordination with relevant agencies, as appropriate.
- *In 2015–2016,* continue to pursue commitments in the WTO rules negotiations to discipline harmful fisheries subsidies and provide greater transparency for fisheries subsidies. Seek to ensure other

WTO Members are more transparent in the notification of their fisheries subsidies.

Lead Agency: USTR

Other Agencies Involved: Coordination with relevant agencies, as appropriate.

- *In 2015–2016,* work to complete and release an updated study reporting on the nature and extent of fisheries subsidies provided by APEC economies, and pursue regional commitments to enhance transparency and efforts to reform fisheries subsidies programs.

  Lead Agencies: USTR, Department of State.

  Other Agencies Involved: Coordination with relevant agencies, as appropriate, including the Department of Commerce.

  When Chile hosts the second Our Ocean Conference in 2015, seek to build on the outcomes of Secretary Kerry's Our Ocean Conference, including by seeking a commitment not to provide subsidies linked to IUU fishing.

  Lead Agencies: USTR, Departments of State and Commerce.

  Other Agencies Involved: Coordination with other relevant agencies, as appropriate.

RECOMMENDATION 6. INTERNATIONAL – CAPACITY BUILDING

Direct the Secretaries of Commerce, Defense, Homeland Security, and State, the Administrator of USAID, and the Attorney General to coordinate with donors, multilateral institutions, and foreign governments and prioritize building capacity to sustainably manage fisheries and combat IUU fishing and seafood fraud.

Rationale

IUU fishing and seafood fraud are global issues that can impact maritime and national security and require a global, concerted effort to combat. Enhancing other countries' capacity for effective fisheries management and enforcement and prosecution of violations can ultimately improve U.S. marine resources. Many less-developed countries lack adequate maritime domain awareness, governance structures, and capable institutions to secure their Exclusive Economic Zone rights and prevent IUU fishing and other activities associated with illegal fishing and trade in illegally harvested fish. Assisting developing countries to strengthen their fisheries governance and enforcement can help regulators in other countries more carefully manage and monitor legitimate fishing and combat IUU fishing practices and help ensure seafood sold in different markets is produced in accordance with the applicable law.

Building capacity and political will to combat IUU fishing will be most successful when we recognize the broader context in which these activities occur, and undertake a strategic and comprehensive approach to fisheries sector reform and address associated criminal activities. IUU fishing and seafood fraud have different impacts that require different capacity building approaches across fishery sectors, including: industrial fisheries, small-scale fisheries, and aquaculture. Effective capacity building will require the use of strategic partnerships, a comprehensive approach to IUU fishing as a development issue, and coordinated delivery of U.S. government support.

Implementation Steps

Lead Agencies: NOAA, Department of State, and USAID.

Other Agencies Involved*:* NOC Committee agencies as appropriate, including USFWS, DOJ, and DHS/ USCG.

- *By May 2015*, NOAA, the Department of State, and USAID will convene an interagency working group consisting of experts from all interested agencies. This group will prioritize capacity building efforts across agencies, with international development organizations and non-federal organizations including coordinating with related efforts under the Presidential Task Force on Wildlife Trafficking, the White House Strategy to Combat Transnational Organized Crime, and the President's Interagency Task Force to Monitor and Combat Trafficking in Persons.
- *By August 2015,* the Department of Justice will form an IUU fishing and seafood fraud multinational advisory body in cooperation with INTERPOL, to inform the aforementioned U.S. interagency working group coordination process by:
- Sharing information regarding multilateral or bilateral priority areas of IUU fishing and seafood fraud investigations.

- Developing mechanisms for coordinated and targeted enforcement or interdiction actions to address priority areas.
- Identifying needed international enforcement tools, and promoting development and implementation of these tools through the capacity building strategic plan to be defined by the interagency working group.
- *By January 2016,* members of the interagency working group, in consultation with relevant donors, governments, technical organizations, industry, and the non-governmental community, will:
- Define priority geographies and seafood species that present the most pressing problems with IUU fishing and seafood fraud.
- Create an ongoing inventory of cooperation and assistance activities to include recently completed, ongoing, and planned activities implemented by the broad community of donors, technical groups, government, and non-governmental organizations working on these issues.
- Complete a review of the types of interventions, best practices, and enforcement tools that have been successful in strengthening fisheries management and eliminating IUU fishing at national, regional, and global scales.
- Encourage external development of innovative tools and technology to address IUU fishing and seafood fraud.
- *By April 2016,* the interagency working group, in consultation with relevant government, donor, technical, industry, and non-governmental organizations and with appropriate public outreach, will develop a strategic, coordinated action plan for building capacity to strengthen fisheries management and eliminate IUU fishing.

RECOMMENDATION 7. INTERNATIONAL – DIPLOMATIC PRIORITY

Direct the Secretary of State to maintain combating IUU fishing and seafood fraud as a diplomatic priority in order to gain the support of senior officials in priority countries to enhance political will for combating IUU fishing and seafood fraud.

Rationale

IUU fishing and seafood fraud are global problems, and no single nation alone can solve them. Diplomacy tools and public outreach can be used to build on key bilateral relationships and encourage our foreign government partners to enhance their efforts to combat IUU fishing and seafood fraud. These issues must continue to be prioritized in our bilateral and multilateral work with other nations and in our public engagement. Building effective coalitions to combat IUU fishing and seafood fraud will also require effective engagement through multilateral organizations and at high-profile, high-level international meetings. Diplomatic efforts will emphasize the negative impacts of IUU fishing and seafood fraud on food and nutrition security, economic security, peace and security, and rule of law.

Implementation Steps

Lead Agency: Department of State.

Other Agencies Involved: NOAA, USTR, USAID, and other NOC Committee agencies as appropriate.

The Task Force agencies will ensure that issues related to implementing a strong international framework to combat IUU fishing and seafood fraud are featured in discussions between senior officials and their foreign counterparts, including those at the foreign affairs, fisheries, finance, trade, and justice ministries. Discussions at the Secretary, Deputy Secretary, and Under Secretary and ambassadorial levels will seek to advance specific priorities related to efforts to combat IUU fishing and seafood fraud, such as ratification of the Port State Measures Agreement, and the overall implementation of the Task Force recommendations. This will facilitate collaboration between our respective technical and enforcement agencies to ensure that illegally caught or fraudulently labeled seafood does not enter U.S. commerce.

Senior Department of State and NOAA officials will seek outcomes that prioritize action to combat IUU fishing and seafood fraud at high-level events in the next 18 months, including:

- The Boston International Seafood Show, March 2015.
- The Third World Ocean Summit, hosted by The Economist, June 2015.

- The 39th Session of the Conference of the UN Food and Agriculture Organization, June 2015.
- The 70th Regular Session of the UN General Assembly, September 2015.
- The Second Our Ocean Conference, hosted by Chile, October 2015.
- The 32nd Session of the FAO Committee on Fisheries, Spring 2016.

The Department of State will coordinate with NOAA, USTR, USAID, and other relevant agencies to develop a strategy *by June 2015* to strengthen embassy advocacy and public diplomacy to increase awareness of issues related to IUU fishing and seafood fraud, and build support for actions for addressing these issues at the national, regional, and global levels, particularly in developing countries. This strategy will include:

- Training modules to prepare embassy officers to engage in IUU fishing and seafood fraud issues effectively.
- Guidance for developing diplomatic demarches and public outreach strategies, including engaging stakeholders and partners.
- Diplomatic demarches.
- A harmonized approach to public diplomacy and public outreach events in support of specific fisheries issues or high-level events over the next 18 months.

RECOMMENDATION 8. ENFORCEMENT – INFORMATION SHARING

Direct the Task Force members, to include the Secretaries of Agriculture, Commerce, Health and Human Services, Homeland Security, and the Interior, and the Attorney General to develop within 180 days a strategy with implementation deadlines to optimize the collection, sharing, and analysis of information and resources to prevent IUU or fraudulently labeled seafood from entering U.S. commerce. This strategy should include a plan to increase support and coordination across agencies for forensic analysis of seafood species and corresponding collection, archiving, and analysis of related reference specimens, as well as reflect efforts to increase coordination with state and local governments per Recommendation 11.

Rationale

Close cooperation among law enforcement organizations at the international, federal, and state/ local levels is utilized to identify and interdict IUU and fraudulently labeled seafood. Maximizing the effectiveness of this collaboration, and further enhancing ongoing cooperation will be necessary to prevent IUU and fraudulently labeled seafood from entering U.S. commerce.

Federal and state agencies have a role in preventing the distribution of IUU seafood products and in detecting and preventing seafood fraud throughout the supply chain. While federal law enforcement agencies cooperate routinely, engagement in the effort to target IUU seafood products and seafood fraud is relatively new for some critical agencies, particularly those at the state and local level. Development of information sharing mechanisms, coordination of joint, intelligence-driven enforcement operations, and development of protocols across agencies to better utilize law enforcement tools, such as forensics, would maximize the effectiveness of limited law enforcement resources to detect and interdict IUU fish and fish products from entering U.S. commerce. Additional coordination and investment in forensic resources will allow greater throughput, decreasing turnaround time for processing of evidence in time-sensitive cases, and allowing more effective targeting of shipments examined for fraud.

This recommendation seeks to expand existing interagency collaboration for information sharing (such as through Customs and Border Protection's Commercial Targeting and Analysis Center (CTAC)), and joint law enforcement operations, as well as formalizing new protocols for cooperation on sharing of expertise in necessary enforcement tools, such as forensics.

Implementation Steps

Lead Agencies: NOAA, DHS/CBP, and DOJ.

Other Agencies Involved: DHS/ICE, DHS/USCG, FDA, USDA, USFWS, DOS, DOD.

- *By May 2015,* complete an inventory of existing interagency agreements, joint activities, and ongoing/ planned operations that may be utilized under this recommendation. This would include identification of existing facilities for conducting forensic analysis and their capabilities. In addition, identify any necessary amendments to or modifications of existing agreements, or the need for new agreements, and pursue them. Finally, the inventory should make allowance for inclusion of relevant MDA tools identified pursuant to Recommendation 3. This inventory is necessary to determine gaps in collaboration and cooperation on information sharing.

- *By September 2015,* finalize a strategy to optimize the collection, sharing, and analysis of information and resources to prevent IUU or fraudulently labeled seafood from entering U.S. commerce and circulate to the NOC Committee. Present to state and local law enforcement personnel and stakeholders as appropriate. The strategy will include sub-groups to develop focused input on:
- Information sharing to include DHS assets such as CBP's Commercial Targeting and Analysis Center (CTAC) and expanded access to information across all relevant enforcement agencies including MDA tools developed pursuant to Recommendation 3, trend information on fraudulent seafood that may be collected under Customs Mutual Assistance Agreements pursuant to Recommendation 9, and information collected from the traceability program collected pursuant to Recommendations 14 and 15.
- Protocols, procedures, and agreements for joint enforcement operations targeting IUU fish and fish product as well as seafood fraud.
- Procedures for interagency cooperation on: 1) use and development of forensic tools, including means to fill existing gaps in capabilities and eliminate duplication; 2) procedures for when/how resources of one agency can be accessed and utilized by partner agencies; 3) development of specific forensic analysis information required by each agency to promote effective enforcement actions by any or all agencies; and 4) cataloging resources, aligning product codes and taxonomies pursuant to Recommendation 10, and for example, obtaining reference specimens and test results.
- Mechanisms/processes for coordination, information sharing and development of proposed joint operations to include appropriate federal, state, and local law enforcement agencies.

RECOMMENDATION 9. ENFORCEMENT – CUSTOMS MUTUAL ASSISTANCE AGREEMENTS

Direct the Secretary of Homeland Security to leverage existing and future Customs Mutual Assistance Agreements (CMAAs) to exchange relevant information and encourage foreign customs administrations to cooperate in combating illegal, unreported, and unregulated (IUU) fishing and seafood fraud.

Rationale

While there is significant information available related to domestic seafood product, there is often a lack of information readily available for seafood products in international commerce, including farmed products and fish processed at sea. The United States needs to leverage its existing resources and available tools to facilitate the sharing of information to close this gap and ensure that law enforcement personnel have the information they need to take action to prevent the fraudulent importation of seafood into the United States.

DHS has broad authorities to share and exchange information and cooperate with domestic and international partners to combat customs violations, including the fraudulent importation of fish and seafood, and illegal imports of fish and seafood originating from IUU fishing activities as they relate to customs violations. CMAAs are essential tools that provide the legal framework for the exchange of information, documents, and other mutual assistance that aid the United States and its partners in the prevention, detection, and investigation of customs offenses.

The United States currently has 73 bilateral CMAAs with customs administrations around the world. CMAAs are jointly negotiated and implemented by U.S. Customs and Border Protection (CBP) and U.S. Immigration and Customs Enforcement (ICE) within DHS. As CBP and ICE have broad authorities to enforce federal laws at the border, information sharing under CMAAs can extend to include information pertaining to fraudulent and other illegal importations of fish and seafood. Additionally, CMAAs establish the foundational framework for further customs-to-customs engagement between the Parties on specific issues. More information on

CMAAs can be found here: http://www.cbp.gov/border-security/ international-initiatives/international-agreements/cmaa.

Implementation Steps

Lead Agency: DHS.

The United States is eager to increase our information sharing abilities via CMAAs to deter customs violations, collect revenue, and facilitate lawful trade. DHS, working with other agencies as appropriate, will leverage CMAAs to support investigations of seafood fraud and of imports originating from IUU fishing as they relate to customs violations, to support risk-based targeting of illicit seafood shipments, and to facilitate further cooperation with foreign governments to encourage the development of best practices to prevent illicit commodities and shipments from entering U.S. commerce long before they reach U.S. borders.

- Immediately begin to highlight its increased focus on combating fraudulently imported fish and seafood, whether wild-caught or farmed, and IUU fishing as it relates to customs violations, working closely with its partners, particularly in those regions where fraudulently imported seafood originates.
- On an ongoing basis, work with NOC Committee partner agencies, pursuant to the strategy developed under Recommendation 8, partners under the Commercial Targeting Analysis Center (CTAC), and partners in the ICE Homeland Security Investigations (HSI) Trade Transparency Unit (TTU), to identify the gaps in information exchanged across customs and enforcement agencies and take action on those areas where it can use its authorities and agreements to achieve the most effective enforcement.

RECOMMENDATION 10. ENFORCEMENT – SPECIES NAME AND CODE

Direct the Secretaries of Agriculture, Commerce, Health and Human Services, and Homeland Security, with input from the Attorney General, to standardize and clarify rules on identifying the species, common name, and origin of seafood. Direct the Secretaries of Commerce and Homeland Security and the U.S. Trade Representative to work with the International Trade Commission to adjust U.S. tariff codes to enhance identification in trade of species subject to IUU fishing or seafood fraud accordingly. The agencies should aim to publish these revised rules and adjusted codes not later than one year after the adoption of this recommendation.

Rationale

A wide variety of finfish and shellfish products are consumed by the American public, amounting to about 15 pounds per capita annually, with the majority imported. Whether imported or domestically produced, seafood products should not be marketed to consumers in a way that is false or misleading. For classification of imports, codes and descriptions are assigned to seafood products under the Harmonized Tariff Schedule (HTS) of the United States which is maintained by the U.S. International Trade Commission (ITC). In addition, the FDA maintains a list of product codes to describe seafood commodities entered into U.S. commerce. The FDA product codes refer to fish name, packaging, and type of processing. Deliberate misrepresentation of the species in trade can defraud consumers and allow the infiltration of the products of IUU fishing into the supply chain. Increasing the specificity of HTS codes, and names could help address issues of proper identification of seafood products in trade. Such specificity will help enforcement officials focus limited resources on shipments more likely to contain IUU seafood as well as help to protect against seafood fraud.

Implementation Steps

Lead Agencies: NOAA, DHS/CBP, and FDA
Other agencies involved: USTR, USFWS, DOJ, USDA and ITC

- *By April 2015,* the lead agencies will convene an interagency technical working group for the purpose of implementing this recommendation.
- *By August 2015,* the Working Group will catalogue the existing rules on identifying the species, name, and origin of seafood entering into

commerce in the United States and determine where standardization or clarification of these rules would help to address problems of IUU fishing and seafood fraud. For those areas where the Working Group determines standardization or clarification of the rules is appropriate, the Working Group will prepare recommendations on how those rules should be standardized or clarified. These recommendations will include, where appropriate, which codes should be adjusted and at what level adjustments are needed, and whether common, market, and/or scientific names should be utilized. Such recommendations will be referred to the ITC and FDA as appropriate.

- *By August 2015,* the Working Group will also consider how the current list of U.S. tariff codes for seafood can be adjusted, including by increasing product specificity, to facilitate identification of species susceptible to IUU fishing or seafood fraud, in support of efforts to keep such products out of U.S. commerce. The Working Group will develop recommendations as to what adjustments should be made and will share them with ITC and FDA and integrate them into the strategy developed pursuant to Recommendation 8.
- *By December 2015,* FDA and other relevant agencies shall standardize and clarify rules on identifying the species, common name, and origin of seafood and adjust U.S. tariff codes to enhance identification in trade of species subject to IUU fishing or seafood fraud based on the recommendations of the Working Group, including with the publication of proposed revisions to any rules *by March 2016.*

RECOMMENDATION 11. ENFORCEMENT – STATE AND LOCAL

Direct the Secretaries of Agriculture, Commerce, Health and Human Services, and Homeland Security, and the Attorney General to work with state and local enforcement authorities to expand information sharing and develop tools that address illegal fishing and seafood fraud at the state and local level.

Rationale

State and local enforcement authorities have long played an important role in combating illegal fishing and seafood fraud. In regulating fisheries through enforcement in state waters and working with NOAA, monitoring landings of fish harvested in federal waters, state and local authorities are often the first recipients of information regarding potential illegal activity and illegally harvested products. They are a vital source of information for federal enforcement agencies and a critical component of fisheries enforcement. In many places, federal agencies already cooperate with state and local authorities on enforcement actions dealing with fisheries violations. For example, NOAA has a Cooperative Enforcement Program (CEP) in place with 27 state and territorial law enforcement agencies, which provide those agencies with the training and authority to enforce federal marine resource laws. DOIUSFWS also has a CEP in place with 47 state and territorial law enforcement agencies, which provide those agencies with the training and authority to enforce federal wildlife laws. Likewise, the Department of Justice (DOJ) frequently works with state and local law enforcement officials on investigations and prosecutions, and has helped establish regional environmental crimes task forces that help foster valuable information sharing and other efficiency building coordination.

State and local authorities also play a key role in detecting and preventing seafood fraud, since intrastate seafood sales, including those at the restaurant and retail level, are regulated by state and local, rather than federal, authorities. Agencies such as the FDA contract with state and local authorities that inspect retail and food establishments to carry out inspections at facilities under FDA's jurisdiction. State and local authorities thus benefit from FDA training and information regarding seafood inspections and species designations.

Implementation Steps

Lead Agencies: NOAA and DOJ.
Other Agencies Involved: FDA, USFWS.

- *By June 2015,* NOAA Fisheries Office of Law Enforcement (OLE) will prioritize combating seafood fraud and the sale of IUU seafood products for joint federal/state enforcement operations under its CEP. Actions to reflect this prioritization would include:

- Providing IUU fishing and seafood fraud–specific enforcement trainings on a semi-annual basis with state and local personnel, including inspectors and investigators.
- Developing online training modules and technical assistance (e.g., assistance to increase species identification capabilities) to help law enforcement recognize and document potential IUU fishing and seafood fraud issues.
- Developing procedures for expanded information sharing and access to NOAA OLE fisheries intelligence analysts for law enforcement partners under the CEP.
- Committing NOAA enforcement officers and special agent resources as appropriate to investigating potential seafood fraud and IUU seafood products violations.
- *In 2015,* DOJ will prioritize investigation and prosecution of cases involving IUU fishing and seafood fraud in coordinated efforts, including with U.S. Attorneys' Offices and the relevant regional environmental crimes task forces. These efforts will include NOAA CEP state enforcement representatives.
- *By April 2015,* DOJ will designate contact points for fisheries agents to directly speak with and obtain support from specialized prosecutors about ongoing investigations or referrals related to seafood fraud and illegal fishing.
- *By May 2015,* DOJ's Environmental Crimes Policy Committee will explore ways to engage U.S. Attorney's Offices on the need to prioritize seafood fraud and illegal fishing cases.
- *By July 2015,* DOJ will explore ways and means to conduct a pilot judicial training workshop regarding both fisheries and wildlife cases, with a goal, if those explorations are productive, of conducting a limited pilot workshop during 2015.
- The negotiated FDA state food safety inspection contracts to be awarded in *FY 2016* will include a focus area on mislabeling and seafood species substitution issues. FDA will conduct training with state contractors and encourage information sharing of mislabeling and seafood species substitution issues beginning *in FY 2015.*

RECOMMENDATION 12.
ENFORCEMENT – ENFORCEMENT AUTHORITIES

Work with Congress to the extent necessary to broaden agency enforcement authorities, including those to 1) search, inspect, and seize seafood, both at the point of entry into U.S. commerce (whether from foreign or domestic sources) and throughout the supply chain; and 2) pursue a full range of judicial enforcement options for trafficking and other violations related to IUU fishing and seafood fraud.

Rationale

Agencies need to leverage existing authorities through stronger coordination and, where necessary, seek additional enforcement tools to address growing concerns over IUU fishing and seafood fraud, in particular the illegal entry of seafood products into U.S. commerce. At present, there are crucial gaps in federal authorities that prevent agencies from monitoring the entirety of the seafood supply chain. Although NOAA has responsibility for implementing and enforcing an increasing number of U.S. obligations related to implementation of catch documentation and trade tracking schemes, many of NOAA's existing enforcement authorities are focused on at-sea and dockside enforcement that is more appropriate to the enforcement of harvesting violations. DHS (CBP and ICE HSI), FDA, NOAA, and USDA have robust regulatory authorities applicable at the point of entry of seafood, and USDA has additional authorities at the point of food processing. However, to more effectively curb the entry of IUU and fraudulently marketed seafood products into U.S. commerce, agencies need the ability to inspect and verify the legality of fish and fish product throughout the supply chain. For example the Magnuson-Stevens Fishery Conservation and Management Act (MSA) prohibits the import of fish taken in violation of foreign law but effective enforcement of this prohibition requires the cooperation and coordination with border control agencies such as ICE HSI and CBP.

Tools such as increased penalties and administrative and judicial enforcement mechanisms are also vital to combating IUU fishing and seafood fraud. However, a number of key statutory authorities that deal with IUU fishing and seafood fraud do not have adequate penalties or administrative and judicial mechanisms, while others that could be used expressly exempt fisheries violations. For example, the Lacey Act, which prohibits the importation of fish and fish products taken or imported in violation of a foreign law or treaty, and the Antarctic Living Marine Resources Convention Act, both have very low civil penalty maximums. In addition, many of the statutes implementing international fisheries agreements have limited criminal provisions that are not applicable to the harvest or trade of fish, but only to conduct such as assault, harassment, obstruction, and false statement. Tools such as increased civil monetary penalties, clear forfeiture authority, and increased authority to impose criminal fines and penalties, including through the application of laws related to money laundering and the Racketeer Influenced and Corrupt Organizations Act (RICO), are needed to deter illegal activity motivated by the large profits that may be associated with IUU fishing and trade in the resulting product. ICE HSI and CBP can leverage their existing Title 19 seizure and forfeiture authorities, and ICE HSI can leverage its authority and jurisdiction over criminal customs violations as specified unlawful activities under the Money Laundering Control Act and as predicate offenses under RICO. If collaboration with ICE HSI or CBP is not possible, these tools would provide law enforcement officials within other agencies and prosecutors with greater ability to punish illegal activity with penalties that provide an effective deterrent.

Implementation Steps

Agencies involved: NOAA, DOJ, DHS/CBP, DHS/ICE, and other NOC Committee agencies as relevant.

- Review pending investigations and enforcement actions and leverage other agencies' authorities for successful outcomes.
- Continue to work with Congress to identify and propose necessary law enforcement tools and to strengthen and pass legislation to address IUU fishing and seafood fraud.
- *By July 2015,* NOAA and DOJ will hold briefings for key Congressional Committees, Members, Caucuses, and staff with agency leadership, as well as enforcement experts and stakeholders, to explain the rationale and need for appropriate enforcement tools to combat IUU fishing and seafood fraud.
- Use existing fora such as Capitol Hill Oceans Week in June 2015 to continue to educate Congressional members, staff, and constituents

about IUU fishing, seafood fraud, and the need to enhance enforcement authorities.

RECOMMENDATION 13. PARTNERSHIPS – FORUM

Direct the Task Force to establish a regular forum with harvesters, importers, dealers, retailers, processors, and non-governmental organizations to enhance collaboration in combating IUU fishing and seafood fraud and to improve understanding of the levels and nature of IUU fishing and seafood fraud and related criminal activities.

Rationale

Just as one federal agency alone cannot combat IUU fishing and seafood fraud, these issues cannot be addressed only by the federal or state governments. It is important that the federal agencies join forces and take strong steps in partnership with the non-federal entities such as harvesters, importers, dealers, retailers, processors, academia, and non-governmental organizations. In particular, the wide range of entities that provided public comments on both the establishment of the Task Force and the implementation of its recommendations demonstrates a broad knowledge and investment made in addressing these issues across the seafood supply chain. As federal efforts to address issues related to IUU fishing and seafood fraud continue, it is crucial to bring together all relevant stakeholders so that the NOC Committee has a range of experience and collaborative resources to draw upon and inform federal policy. From this regular forum, areas of collaboration between federal agencies and stakeholders can be identified to address IUU fishing and seafood fraud concerns in the supply chain. A number of initiatives and professional fora external to the federal government already exist to bring together various stakeholders and collaborate on a wide range of fisheries issues. It is important to build upon and engage in these venues as an opportunity to continue robust dialogue and engagement with interested stakeholders.

Taking this context into account, the NOC Committee will establish a regular forum open to all interested stakeholders to facilitate discussion and exchange information on combating IUU fishing and seafood fraud. Comprised of both virtual and in-person components, this forum would, among other things, enhance public awareness of NOC Committee activities, as well as highlight non-government efforts to combat IUU fishing and seafood fraud, and develop public-private partnerships. This forum would not supplant formal comment periods for specific regulatory proposals or policies that are developed in response to other Task Force recommendations, but could serve as a feedback loop as the NOC Committee implements recommendations as well as help provide innovative ideas and solutions moving forward.

Implementation Steps

Lead Agency: NOAA
Other Agencies Involved: All NOC Committee agencies

The forum will manifest in a few different ways:

- NOC Committee agencies will develop and maintain a public web portal to facilitate the work of the forum *by December 2015.* Among other things, this web portal will:
- Serve as a repository of information on relevant laws, regulations, and policies related to IUU fishing and seafood fraud.
- Link to the websites and relevant pages of NOC Committee agencies.
- Provide contact information of NOC Committee agencies.
- Provide a mechanism to report IUU Fishing and seafood fraud complaints.
- Serve as a public web portal to inform stakeholders and other interested parties about various NOC Committee engagement events and related federal activities throughout the year.
- Provide other related NOC Committee information, as relevant.
- Hold an annual, public, in-person forum of interested stakeholders that may focus its discussions on a specific IUU fishing or seafood fraud concern. Topic suggestions will be solicited throughout the year at various NOC Committee engagement sessions and through the public web portal. *By December 2015,* the first in-person forum will be held, with a focus on the implementation of particular Task Force recommendations of interest to stakeholders (to be determined through stakeholder engagement).

- To support these in-person meetings, the NOC Committee will develop a series of ongoing virtual meetings such as webinars to exchange information on implementation of Task Force recommendations and on the roles of NOC Committee agencies, and to solicit public feedback. A first virtual meeting will take place *in June 2015.*
- NOC Committee representatives will regularly engage at other stakeholder forums throughout the year to apprise stakeholders of ongoing NOC Committee efforts and receive feedback. Such forums could include: conferences and industry trade shows organized by entities external to the government, various Regional Fishery Management Council meetings, and Capitol Hill Ocean Week, among others.

RECOMMENDATIONS 14 AND 15. TRACEABILITY – TRACEABILITY PROGRAM

Direct the Task Force, with input from U.S. industry and other stakeholders, to identify and develop within six months a list of the types of information and operational standards needed for an effective seafood traceability program to combat seafood fraud and IUU seafood in U.S. commerce.

Direct the Task Force to establish, within 18 months, the first phase of a risk-based traceability program to track seafood from point of harvest to entry into U.S. commerce.

Rationale

It is in the national interest to prevent the entry of illegal goods, including illegally harvested or produced seafood, into U.S. commerce. Creating an integrated program that better facilitates data collection, sharing, and analysis among relevant regulators and enforcement authorities would be a significant step forward in addressing IUU fishing and seafood fraud. The federal government will work with states, industry, and other stakeholders to develop and implement this program, consistent with U.S. international legal obligations, including U.S, obligations under the World Trade Organization Agreement.

First, the federal government will need to define the types of information to be collected regarding seafood sold in the United States and the operational standards to be applied to the collection, retention, and transmission of such information, such as electronic collection wherever possible. This program should be developed in a way that permits all authorized agencies to enter, analyze, use, and verify the data while still protecting information consistent with statutory authorities. NOAA and its fishery management partners already collect much of this information for many species for use in domestic fisheries management. Also, at the border the FDA collects information on the identity of imported seafood products, harvested or farmed. CBP is able to utilize its authorities at the border to enforce other U.S. agency requirements for imported seafood products, while ICE has the authority to investigate cross-border violations. It will be critical to this effort to knit together the information collected by these agencies and others and leverage their respective authorities, while ensuring that other federal agencies have access to that information and identifying the domestic and international gaps in information.

The program will initially be applied to seafood products of particular concern because the species at issue are subject to significant seafood fraud or because they are at significant risk of being caught by IUU fishing (referred to in this recommendation as "at risk" species). The federal government will first need to outline the criteria and principles to determine which species currently face these risks, as well as to understand whether additional data need to be collected for these species, and develop a strategy to collect those data. Once the steps outlined on pages 37-39 have been implemented, the NOC Committee will evaluate the program's development and use lessons learned to outline next steps required for eventually expanding the program to other seafood entering U.S. commerce. The NOC Committee will again evaluate progress in implementing the program and the steps outlined in the previous report after one full year of program implementation. As set forth in the *Federal Register* notice that relayed the Task Force's recommendations to the President, it is the goal of the U.S. government "to eventually expand the program to all seafood at first point of sale or import." The process for expansion will account for, among other factors, consideration of authorities needed, stakeholder input, and the cost-effectiveness of program expansion. The NOC Committee will also consider how certain types of information within the traceability system (e.g., species, geographic origin, means of production (such as wild-caught versus aquaculture), and gear type) could be made available to the consumer.

Implementation Steps

The NOC Committee intends to take steps to develop this program in six key areas: 1) developing types of information/operational standards related to data collection; 2) determining species currently "at risk" to IUU fishing and seafood fraud, 3) analyzing what data are collected and the gaps in data; 4) sharing information within the federal government and with consumers, as allowable by law; 5) establishing a trusted trader program; and 6) evaluating and expanding the overall program. As noted above, implementing these steps will require engagement from several members of the NOC Committee but coordinated implementation of authorities held by CBP, NOAA, and FDA will be especially critical. Some steps will be concurrent and some will need to be sequential. The notes after each heading indicate where in the process each step is expected to be implemented.

- Types of Information and Operational Standards – April through September 2015: The information collected will include the following information: who harvested or produced the fish (e.g., name and flag State of harvesting vessel and/or farm facility, type of fishing gear); what species was harvested (e.g., species name, form, and quantity of the product); where and when the seafood was harvested and landed (e.g., ocean area of catch, farm location, date of harvest, date/point of first landing). The operational standards under each of the categories above should also draw upon and utilize applicable experience, best practices, and existing standards where possible. Operational standards may include things such as how data is to be collected, in what format, who would collect the data, data verification processes, and data security, among others.
- By June 2015, the NOC Committee will put out a proposal for the minimum types of information, as well as operational standards for a 30-day public comment period. By September 2015, the NOC Committee will finalize recommendations in this regard for appropriate agency action.
- *Identifying Current At Risk Species Threatened by IUU Fishing and Seafood Fraud* – April through October 2015: The Secretaries of Commerce, Health and Human Services, State, and any other relevant agencies will identify certain species of fish or seafood that are presently of particular concern because they are currently subject to

significant seafood fraud or because they are at significant risk of being caught by IUU fishing.

- The NOC Committee will start a two-month effort to engage the public to gather input on what principles we should use to determine what species are "at risk."
- *By July 2015,* within two months after the end of the aforementioned public engagement, the NOC Committee will release proposed principles for evaluating whether species are "at risk," as well as a proposed list of species for a 30-day public comment period.
- *By October 2015,* two months after the end of the public comment session, the NOC Committee will finalize recommendations both with respect to the principles as well as the list of species that are "at risk" for appropriate agency action.
- *Data Collection – Determining Gaps* – October 2015 through January 2016: The Secretaries of Homeland Security, HHS, and Commerce, and other federal agencies, states, and other partners, as appropriate, will work together to determine data collection needs for these "at-risk" species.
- There will be a number of species for which we already collect the necessary data. For those species that need additional data collected, within 3 months of the "at-risk" list of species being finalized, the federal government will develop a strategy to collect this data including working with Regional Fishery Management Councils for domestically managed species and working through RFMOs for those species managed by those organizations.
- *Additional Point of Entry Data Collection* – October 2015 through September 2016: Based on the results of the gap analysis, the Department of Commerce (NOAA), in consultation with Departments of Homeland Security (CBP), Health and Human Services (FDA), and Treasury, as lead for the International Trade Data System (ITDS)/Single Window, shall, if there is need for additional data to be collected, initiate a rulemaking to collect additional information electronically as a requisite of entry into U.S. commerce for at-risk species. This rulemaking would propose types of information outlined above to accompany shipments of seafood at their point of entry into U.S. commerce.
- The final rule will be issued *by August 2016* in order for it to be effective *by September 2016.*

- *Information Sharing* – October 2015 through November 2016: Information collected will be shared among federal regulatory and law enforcement agencies for analysis and other relevant actions to prevent IUU or fraudulently marketed seafood from entering U.S. commerce pursuant to the strategy developed by the Secretaries of Agriculture, Commerce, Health and Human Services, Homeland Security, and the Interior, and the Attorney General (see Recommendation 8 for additional information).
- *By July 2016,* work with our non-federal partners who have data collection systems to ensure MOUs and other similar documents are in place to ensure data can be shared with federal law enforcement agencies.
- *Trusted Trader Program* – April 2015 through September 2016: The Secretary of Commerce will collaborate with the Secretary of Homeland Security and other agencies as relevant to assist in developing a voluntary Commerce Trusted Trader Program for importers of these identified species. The Program will provide benefits such as reduced targeting and inspections and enhanced streamlined entry into U.S. commerce for certified importers.
- *By March 2016,* DHS and Commerce will propose a voluntary trusted trader program for a two-month public comment period. The program will be finalized *by September 2016.*
- *Evaluation and Further Implementation* – Implementation of this risk-based traceability program for collection of information at the point of entry into U.S. commerce will be evaluated regularly to identify whether it is meeting the intended objectives and how it can be expanded to provide more information to prevent seafood fraud and combat IUU fishing.
- *By December 2016,* the NOC Committee will issue a report that includes an evaluation of the program as implemented to date as well as recommendations of how and under what timeframe it would be expanded. If the program cannot be expanded to all fish at this time, the report will explain why not and lay out a timeline to steps that advance this objective. The report will further update the list of at-risk species developed and lay out additional authorities needed for more robust implementation, and recommend how shareable information within the traceability program (e.g., species, geographic origin, means of harvest or production, and gear type) could be made available to the consumer.

- *By September 2017*, an update and evaluation of the program and next steps as outlined on page 37 will be issued.

CONCLUSION

Where a timeframe is not specifically noted under a recommendation, the relevant agencies will report to the National Ocean Council's standing IUU Fishing/Seafood Fraud Committee on the progress of implementing that recommendation one year from receiving guidance from the President. In addition, recognizing that a valuable and extensive body of information on fisheries and seafood products would be created by the recommendations above, the IUU Fishing/Seafood Fraud Committee will report annually to the President on seafood trends, key issues related to IUU fishing and seafood fraud, and progress on development and implementation of a comprehensive and risk-based traceability program.

In: Action Plan for Combating Illegal … ISBN: 978-1-63483-164-2
Editor: Caleb Jennings

Chapter 2

PRESIDENTIAL MEMORANDUM: COMPREHENSIVE FRAMEWORK TO COMBAT ILLEGAL, UNREPORTED, AND UNREGULATED FISHING AND SEAFOOD FRAUD*

Barack Obama

MEMORANDUM FOR THE HEADS OF EXECUTIVE DEPARTMENTS AND AGENCIES

SUBJECT: Establishing a Comprehensive Framework to Combat Illegal, Unreported, and Unregulated Fishing and Seafood Fraud

The United States is a global leader in sustainable seafood. Over the course of the last 6 years, the United States has largely ended overfishing in federally managed waters and successfully rebuilt a record number of stocks depleted by the excesses of the past. At the same time, effective domestic management and enforcement of fishing regulations have supported near record highs in both landings and revenue for our domestic fishing industry. As a result, the U.S. management scheme is recognized internationally as a model for other countries as they work to end overfishing.

---

* This is an edited, reformatted and augmented version of a presidential memorandum issued by the White House, Office of the Press Secretary, June 17, 2014.

Nevertheless, illegal, unreported, and unregulated (IUU) fishing continues to undermine the economic and environmental sustainability of fisheries and fish stocks, both in the United States and around the world. Global losses attributable to the black market from IUU fishing are estimated to be $10-23 billion annually, weakening profitability for legally caught seafood, fueling illegal trafficking operations, and undermining economic opportunity for legitimate fishermen in the United States and around the world.

It is in the national interest of the United States to promote a framework that supports sustainable fishing practices and combats seafood fraud and the sale of IUU fishing products. To achieve these objectives, the United States will need to enhance the tools it has available to combat IUU fishing and seafood fraud, including by implementing the United Nations Food and Agriculture Organization Agreement on Port State Measures to Prevent, Deter and Eliminate Illegal, Unreported and Unregulated Fishing; strengthening coordination and implementation of existing authorities to combat IUU fishing and seafood fraud; working with the Congress to strengthen and harmonize the enforcement provisions of U.S. statutes for implementing international fisheries agreements; and working with industry and foreign partners to develop and implement new and existing measures, such as voluntary, or other, traceability programs, that can combat IUU fishing and seafood fraud, and ensure accurate labeling for consumers.

Therefore, by the authority vested in me as President by the Constitution and the laws of the United States of America, and to ensure that seafood sold in the United States is legally and sustainably caught and to combat the negative impacts of seafood fraud on the United States, I hereby direct the following:

Section 1. Policy. (a) It shall be the policy of the United States for all executive departments and agencies (agencies) to combat IUU fishing and seafood fraud by strengthening coordination and implementation of relevant existing authorities and, where appropriate, by improving the transparency and traceability of the seafood supply chain. All agencies and offices charged with overseeing the seafood supply chain and verifying the authenticity of its products shall implement and enforce relevant policies, regulations, and laws to ensure that seafood sold in the United States is legally caught and accurately labeled. (b) It shall also be the policy of the United States to promote legally and sustainably caught and accurately labeled seafood and to take appropriate actions within existing authorities and budgets to assist foreign nations in building capacity to combat IUU fishing and seafood fraud. In addition, agencies shall identify opportunities to enhance domestic and international efforts to combat global IUU fishing and seafood fraud.

Sec. 2. Establishment. There is established, as a subcommittee reporting to the National Ocean Council established by Executive Order 13547 of July 19, 2010 (Stewardship of the Ocean, Our Coasts, and the Great Lakes), a Presidential Task Force on Combating Illegal, Unreported, and Unregulated Fishing and Seafood Fraud (Task Force), to be co-chaired by the Secretaries of State and Commerce, or their designees. The Task Force shall meet not later than 60 days from the date of this memorandum and at least quarterly thereafter.

Sec. 3. Membership. In addition to the Co-Chairs, the Task Force shall include designated senior-level representatives from:

(a) the Department of Defense;
(b) the Department of Justice;
(c) the Department of the Interior;
(d) the Department of Agriculture;
(e) the Department of Commerce;
(f) the Department of Health and Human Services;
(g) the Department of Homeland Security;
(h) the Office of Management and Budget;
(i) the Council on Environmental Quality;
(j) the Office of Science and Technology Policy;
(k) the Office of the United States Trade Representative;
(l) the United States Agency for International Development; and
(m) such agencies and offices as the Co-Chairs may, from time to time, designate.

Sec. 4. Functions. Consistent with the authorities and responsibilities of member agencies, the Task Force shall perform the following functions: (a) Not later than 180 days after the date of this memorandum, the Task Force shall report to the President through the National Ocean Council, with recommendations for the implementation of a comprehensive framework of integrated programs to combat IUU fishing and seafood fraud that emphasizes areas of greatest need. The Task Force should consider a broad range of strategies, including implementation of existing programs, and, if appropriate, development of new, voluntary or other, programs for seafood tracking and traceability. In providing these recommendations, the Task Force shall identify:

(i) existing regulatory authorities and make recommendations regarding further authorities that may be warranted;
(ii) enforcement best practices and challenges;
(iii) benefits provided by such a framework, as well as potential impacts on the U.S. fishing industry;
(iv) opportunities to address these issues at the international level through the regional fisheries management organizations as well as bilateral efforts, such as technical assistance and capacity building;
(v) priority actions that will be taken by agencies, including strengthening coordination between Federal, State, local, and foreign agencies; and
(vi) industry approaches that contribute to efforts to combat IUU fishing and seafood fraud, including with respect to seafood traceability and ways to minimize any costs and reporting burdens on small businesses.

(b) Upon receiving guidance from the President on the recommendations developed pursuant to subsection (a) of this section, the Task Force shall begin its implementation of those recommendations and, within 1 year, report to the President, through the National Ocean Council, on its progress.

(c) The Task Force shall also consider the need for other strategies for addressing IUU fishing and seafood fraud and may provide recommendations on the development and enhancement of those strategies.

(d) In undertaking these efforts, the Task Force shall coordinate its efforts with other Presidential initiatives focused on related issues, including the work of the Presidential Task Force on Wildlife Trafficking established in Executive Order 13648 of July 1, 2013 (Combating Wildlife Trafficking), and activities being conducted pursuant to Executive Order 13659 of February 19, 2014 (Streamlining the Export/Import Process for America's Businesses).

(e) The Task Force shall, as applicable, consult with governments at State, local, tribal, and regional levels to achieve the goals and objectives of this memorandum, as well as the private sector, nongovernmental organizations, and academia.

Sec. 5. General Provisions. (a) This memorandum shall be implemented consistent with applicable domestic and international law, and subject to the availability of appropriations.

(b) Nothing in this memorandum shall be construed to impair or otherwise affect:

(i) the authority granted by law to an executive department, agency, or the head thereof; or

(ii) the functions of the Director of the Office of Management and Budget relating to budgetary, administrative, or legislative proposals.

(c) Nothing in this memorandum shall be construed to require the disclosure of confidential business information or trade secrets, classified information, law enforcement sensitive information, or other information that must be protected in the interest of national security or public safety.

(d) This memorandum is not intended to, and does not, create any right or benefit, substantive or procedural, enforceable at law or in equity by any party against the United States, its departments, agencies, or entities, its officers, employees, or agents, or any other person.

BARACK OBAMA

In: Action Plan for Combating Illegal … ISBN: 978-1-63483-164-2
Editor: Caleb Jennings

Chapter 3

SEAFOOD FRAUD*

Harold F. Upton

SUMMARY

Fraudulent seafood sales and marketing—the act of defrauding buyers of seafood for economic gain—has been widely reported and has gained greater public attention in recent years. The extent of seafood fraud is difficult to determine because of its clandestine nature; fraud depends on not being detected, which often depends on not attracting attention or causing immediate harm to customers. Seafood fraud can include a variety of illegal activities, such as transshipping products to avoid antidumping and countervailing duties; mislabeling products or substituting one species for another; overtreating products with water-retaining chemicals; and short-weighting products. Although not illegal, some treatments, such as carbon monoxide/tasteless smoke, are being questioned for their potential to deceive consumers.

The primary federal law that addresses seafood safety and fraud is the Federal Food, Drug, and Cosmetic Act of 1938 (FFDCA; 21 U.S.C. §§301 et seq.). FFDCA prohibits the misbranding or adulteration of food products, including seafood products that have been mislabeled, substituted, or overtreated. FFDCA provides the Food and Drug Administration (FDA) of the Department of Health and Human Services with the primary responsibility for ensuring that domestic and imported

* This is an edited, reformatted and augmented version of a Congressional Research Service publication RL34124, prepared for Members and Committees of Congress, dated April 7, 2015.

foods, including seafood, are safe, wholesome, sanitary, and properly labeled.

Observers have questioned whether greater coordination among federal agencies is needed, whether agency enforcement efforts targeting seafood fraud are sufficient, whether greater authorities are needed to trace seafood from its source to consumers, and whether the penalties for committing seafood fraud are adequate. Some consumer and environmental groups have called on federal agencies to aggressively enforce existing laws and on Congress to pass legislation that targets seafood fraud. Some in the seafood industry have supported industry initiatives to stop seafood fraud, but in most cases they have not advocated for new federal authorities.

On June 17, 2014, President Obama released a presidential memorandum entitled "Comprehensive Framework to Combat Illegal, Unreported, and Unregulated Fishing and Seafood Fraud." The memorandum calls on executive departments and agencies to combat illegal, unreported, and unregulated (IUU) fishing and seafood fraud by strengthening coordination and using existing authorities. The President also established a task force composed of senior-level federal agency representatives to develop recommendations for a comprehensive framework that targets IUU fishing and seafood fraud. On March 15, 2015, the task force released its final recommendations, which included both international and domestic measures. Some segments of the seafood industry have questioned whether IUU fishing and seafood fraud should be addressed as part of the same initiative. They contend that although sometimes related, IUU fishing and seafood fraud are different issues and should be considered separately.

In the 113th Congress, two nearly identical bills, H.R. 1012 and S. 520, were introduced to improve seafood safety and prevent seafood fraud. Both bills would have directed the Departments of Commerce and Health and Human Services to execute a memorandum of understanding to improve agency cooperation. The bills also would have required a standardized list for seafood, improvements to seafood traceability, collection of fraud-related information, more inspections for seafood fraud, and a report to Congress every two years. No actions were taken on either bill during the 113th Congress. To date, no bills that focus on seafood fraud have been introduced in the 114th Congress.

According to the National Oceanic and Atmospheric Administration (NOAA), seafood inspectors have detected fraud in at least 40% of all products submitted to them voluntarily.[1] Media attention to seafood fraud has increased and a variety of schemes to defraud other seafood businesses, retail stores, restaurants, and the public have been reported.[2] These incidents have raised public concern with the identity, value, and safety of seafood. Incidents of seafood fraud have included the following:

- serving lower-priced seafood as higher-priced items;
- marketing mislabeled seafood products;
- transshipping products to avoid antidumping and countervailing duties; and
- overtreating products and labeling seafood packages with inaccurate counts or weights.[3]

Most seafood fraud is based on supplying something different from and inferior to the product that the consumer expects.[4] When consumers purchase a product of lower quality or become aware of seafood substitution, their perception of seafood quality may decrease. In addition, these occurrences may lower consumers' demand for seafood products, and result in economic losses to law-abiding seafood businesses. Seafood fraud also is related to food safety when fish that contain toxins are mislabeled or when fish high in mercury are substituted for another species.

On a broader scale, seafood fraud has been linked to international concerns with illegal, unreported, and unregulated (IUU) fishing.[5] It has been reported that a significant portion of seafood traded in international markets, including seafood imported into the United States, is harvested by IUU fishing activity. On June 17, 2014, President Obama released a presidential memorandum entitled—"Comprehensive Framework to Combat Illegal, Unreported, and Unregulated Fishing and Seafood Fraud."[6] The memorandum calls on executive departments and agencies to use existing authorities to combat IUU fishing and seafood fraud. On March 15, 2015, the task force released its final recommendations, which included both international and domestic measures.[7] However, some segments of the seafood industry have questioned whether IUU fishing and seafood fraud should be addressed as part of the same initiative. They contend that although sometimes related, IUU fishing and seafood fraud are different issues and should be addressed as such.[8]

CONGRESSIONAL INTEREST AND LEGISLATIVE ACTIONS

During the last several Congresses, legislation was introduced to address seafood fraud. In the 113th Congress, two nearly identical bills (H.R. 1012 and S. 520) were designed to strengthen seafood safety and fraud prevention by adopting several different measures. The bills would have required the Secretary of Commerce and the Secretary of Health and Human Services to execute a memorandum of understanding (MOU) to improve agency cooperation on seafood safety and seafood fraud. To improve compliance with existing laws, both bills would have incorporated penalties under provisions of the Magnuson-Stevens Fishery Conservation and Management Act (16 U.S.C. §§1801 et seq.) for violations related to seafood fraud. They also would have required a report to Congress every two years to assess the problem and evaluate progress made to improve seafood safety and prevent seafood fraud. In addition, the bills would have enhanced seafood traceability by requiring the following tracking information for seafood imported into the United States or offered for sale in interstate commerce:

- fishing area in which the fish was caught;
- acceptable market name and scientific name;
- method of harvest;
- date of the catch; and
- weight or number of the individual fish or lot.

No action was taken on either of these bills during the 113th Congress.

In the 112th Congress, S. 50 proposed directing the Departments of Commerce and of Health and Human Services, the Federal Trade Commission, and other federal agencies to combat seafood fraud; the Senate Committee on Commerce, Science, and Transportation reported this bill (S.Rept. 112-131) on January 26, 2012, but no further action was taken. H.R. 6200 sought to address seafood fraud by requiring labels to identify species and origin for both domestic and imported fish and by requiring a plan to coordinate the Food and Drug Administration (FDA) and National Marine Fisheries Service (NMFS) seafood inspections.[9] No further action was taken on H.R. 6200 during the 112th Congress.

Some have questioned whether FDA has sufficient resources to carry out its responsibilities to enforce laws related to seafood fraud. Some believe that FDA requires additional funding to systematically monitor for economic fraud and mislabeling, determine the scope and scale of these types of problems, and develop new programs to address these concerns. They also insist that FDA needs new authorities to facilitate seafood traceability and improve compliance. It remains an open question whether FDA can address seafood fraud using existing authorities and resources or whether new legislation and funding increases will be necessary.

In the 114th Congress, two food safety bills (H.R. 609 and S. 287) and a seafood safety bill (S. 190) have been introduced, but these bills do not address seafood fraud directly. Seafood fraud-related issues that may be considered during the 114th Congress include whether

- federal agencies are collaborating effectively;
- greater authority is needed to improve traceability of seafood through the supply chain;
- penalties for seafood fraud offenses are a deterrent; and
- resources for federal agency detection and enforcement are sufficient.

LAWS AND AGENCY RESPONSIBILITIES

The Federal Food, Drug, and Cosmetic Act and the Fair Packaging and Labeling Act

The primary federal law that addresses mislabeling and safety of food is the Federal Food, Drug, and Cosmetic Act of 1938 (FFDCA; 21 U.S.C. §§301 et seq.).[10] FFDCA requires that foods be safe, wholesome, and accurately labeled. It gives FDA authority over most food regulation (except for most meats and poultry) and includes[11]

- a series of definitions elaborating on the concepts of adulteration and misbranding;
- control over all labeling of foods traveling in interstate commerce;
- detailed regulation of issues concerned with safety and wholesomeness of foods; and
- enforcement remedies available to the agency, when needed.[12]

FFDCA prohibits introducing adulterated or misbranded food into commerce, adulterating or misbranding food that is in commerce, and the receipt and delivery of adulterated or misbranded food in commerce.[13] An article is deemed *misbranded* if, among other things, its labeling is false or misleading or it is offered for sale under the name of another food.[14] A food is deemed *adulterated* "if any substance has been substituted wholly or in part."[15] Under FFDCA, species substitution violates FDA's prohibition against adulteration. For example, the marketing of a less valuable fish as one of higher value is substitution and can result in a finding of adulteration.

The Fair Packaging and Labeling Act (FPLA; 15 U.S.C. §§1451 et seq.) requires that consumers of packaged commodities be provided with accurate information as to their contents. FPLA requires each package label to identify the commodity; the name of its manufacturer, packer, or distributor; and the net quantity of contents, in terms of weight or mass, measure, or numerical count.[16] Congress passed FPLA to "enable consumers to obtain accurate information as to the quantity of the contents and to facilitate value comparisons."[17] Under FPLA, it is unlawful for persons engaged in labeling or packaging of consumer commodities "to distribute or to cause to be distributed in commerce any such commodity if such commodity is contained in a package, or if there is affixed to that commodity a label, which does not conform to the provisions" of the act.[18] Food products falling within the scope of FFDCA that are introduced into interstate commerce in violation of FPLA and its regulations are deemed to be misbranded within the meaning of FFDCA.[19]

FDA has issued regulations that outline general principles for common or usual names of food. The common or usual name must

> accurately identify or describe, in as simple and direct terms as possible, the basic nature of the food or its characterizing properties or ingredients. The name shall be uniform among all identical or similar products and may not be confusingly similar to the name of any other food that is not reasonably encompassed within the same name. Each class or subclass of food shall be given its own common or usual name that states, in clear terms, what it is in a way that distinguishes it from different foods.[20]

A common or usual name of a food may be established by common usage or by regulation.[21] For example, FDA promulgated a regulation establishing that Pacific whiting or North Pacific whiting is the common or usual name of the food fish *Merluccius productus*.[22] Most common or usual names, however, are established through common usage.

Food and Drug Administration

FDA is the primary agency responsible for ensuring that food sold in interstate commerce is safe and properly labeled.[23] The agency's jurisdiction includes seafood, and the agency operates a regulatory program for nearly all fish and fishery products.[24] FDA's program includes research, inspection, compliance, enforcement, and development of regulations and outreach.[25] Responsibility for a food product's safety, wholesomeness, identity, and economic integrity rests with the processor or importer, which must comply with the FDA's regulations promulgated under FFDCA and FPLA.

FDA has the authority to take both administrative and judicial enforcement actions.[26] FDA administrative actions may include inspections, warning letters, recalls, suspension of registration, and administrative detention. For example, agency personnel may detain or temporarily hold food being imported into the United States while it determines if the product is misbranded or adulterated. Judicial actions require some involvement by the courts and may include seizures of violative products, injunctions, criminal prosecutions, and civil penalties.[27] For example, FDA has the authority to take legal actions against sellers of misbranded and adulterated seafood by recommending criminal prosecution or injunction of responsible firms and individuals.[28]

Customs and Border Protection

Customs and Border Protection (CBP) enforces regulations at ports of entry including labeling requirements under FFDCA and the Tariff Act of 1930 (19 U.S.C. §§ 1202 et seq.).[29] The Tariff Act requires all imported articles to be marked with the country of origin for the ultimate purchaser, the last person who will receive the article in the form in which it was imported. However, if the article will undergo substantial transformation, then the processor is considered the ultimate purchaser.[30] CBP is responsible for assessing and collecting the final customs duties on imports. CBP reviews seafood import documentation to detect whether firms are transshipping products to avoid paying import or customs duties. Transshipping seafood is illegal whenever it circumvents trade laws and other applicable trade restrictions.[31] The applicable law and regulation may vary, depending upon trade agreements existing between the United States and specific countries as well as the status of any antidumping and countervailing duties currently in force for particular products imported from designated nations.

National Oceanic and Atmospheric Administration

The National Oceanic and Atmospheric Administration (NOAA) operates a voluntary fee-forservice seafood inspection program under the authority of the Agricultural Marketing Act of 1946 (7 U.S.C. §§1621 et seq.).[32] The program focuses on product quality and offers services to assure compliance with all applicable food regulations. Specific program services include sanitation inspection, system and process audits, product inspection and grading, product lot inspection, laboratory analysis, training, and export certification. Products are evaluated with regard to their general condition and wholesomeness and may be sampled for chemical and microbiological contamination, decomposition, and species identification. Vessels, processing facilities, and retail establishments may receive services for all edible product forms, such as whole fish and products that have undergone varying degrees of processing as well as fish meal products used for animal feeds.

NOAA, FDA, and CBP also enforce provisions of the Lacey Act (16 U.S.C. §3372(d)).[33] Under the Lacy Act, it is illegal to falsely label fish sold in interstate or foreign commerce.[34] NOAA's Office of Law Enforcement sometimes uses this authority to undertake seafood fraud investigations. For example, a NOAA enforcement case involved the purchasing and reselling of farm-raised catfish and Lake Victoria perch as higher-valued grouper, sole, or snapper.[35]

U.S. Department of Agriculture

With passage of the 2002 farm bill (P.L. 107-171; the Farm Security and Rural Investment Act of 2002), country-of-origin labeling (COOL) became mandatory for wild and farm-raised seafood products.[36] The Agriculture Marketing Service (AMS) of the U.S. Department of Agriculture (USDA) is responsible for administration and enforcement of COOL. In October 2004, AMS promulgated an interim final rule requiring certain retailers and their suppliers to notify customers of the country of origin of wild and farm-raised fish and shellfish.[37] COOL does not apply to seafood imports that are processed food items.[38] AMS published final rules to fully implement the country-of-origin requirements on January 15, 2009.[39] USDA has entered into agreements with states having existing enforcement infrastructure to assist in compliance reviews for fish and shellfish.

The 2008 farm bill (P.L. 110-246; the Food, Conservation and Energy Act of 2008) moved responsibility for catfish inspection to USDA by designating catfish as an *amenable species*. As an amenable species, catfish and catfish products are subject to continuous inspection by USDA's Food Safety and Inspection Service (FSIS). Previously, FDA had primary responsibility for the safety of all domestic and imported seafood, including catfish, under FFDCA. The 2008 farm bill also required that the Secretary define the species of catfish that would be inspected by USDA. The definition could be either narrow, such as the family Ictaluridae (North American catfishes), or broad, including all catfish in the order Siluriformes (36 families including North American and Asian catfishes).[40] The broad definition would affect catfish imports because the non-Ictaluridae (Siluriformes from Asia) would be subject to FSIS inspection requirements. The proposed rule provided background related to the catfish inspection but deferred the definition of catfish to the final rule. [41] The final rule was not finalized before debate began on the 2014 farm bill. The 2014 farm bill (P.L. 113-79; the Agricultural Act of 2014) defined catfish as all fish in the order Siluriformes and required USDA to finalize regulations for food safety inspections of catfish no later than 60 days after enactment of the law. As of February 1, 2015, the catfish rule had not been published in the *Federal Register*. The 2014 farm bill also required USDA and FDA to execute an MOU to improve interagency cooperation on food safety and fraud prevention. The MOU was finalized in April 2014.

State Regulation of Seafood Labeling

In addition to federal requirements, states regulate the labeling and branding of seafood under state versions of FFDCA. For example, in Alaska "no person may label or offer for sale any food fish product designated as halibut, with or without additional descriptive words, unless the food fish product is *Hippoglossus* or *Hippoglossus stenolepsis*."[42] In California, an individual who sells any commodity in less quantity than what is represented is guilty of a misdemeanor offense.[43]

Often federal and state agencies coordinate efforts to enforce seafood safety and fraud standards. For example, state agencies, the shellfish industry, FDA, NOAA, and the Environmental Protection Agency work cooperatively under the National Shellfish Sanitation Program (NSSP). NSSP promotes the sanitary control of shellfish produced and sold for human consumption. Foreign governments also participate in NSSP through international agreements with FDA. NSSP provides program guidelines, state growing area classification, and dealer certification programs. One of the main objectives of NSSP is to ensure shellfish are not harvested from polluted waters. This standard is especially important for species of shellfish such as clams and oysters that are often consumed raw.

FRAUDULENT OR DECEPTIVE PRACTICES

Mislabeling or Substituting Species

Substituting an inexpensive species for one of higher value can be relatively easy. The differences in the taste and texture of different fish species' flesh may be subtle, and therefore it is frequently difficult to identify a species in fillet form, especially after it is prepared for consumption. It is difficult to generalize on the occurrence of misidentified species because the practice varies significantly by species, product form, and region. Further, the success of those who perpetrate seafood fraud depends on not being caught and maintaining the deception as long as possible.

Most independent reports indicate that the level of fraud can be significant. For example, a *Consumer Reports* study of seafood sampled from New York, New Jersey, and Connecticut found that 20% to 25% of seafood products were mislabeled.[44] The Los Angeles County Department of Public Health conducted a cooperative survey of seafood substitution made by businesses selling seafood. The survey found that of 103 retail food facilities (66 restaurants and 37 food markets), 74% had seafood label misbranding or false and/or misleading advertisement on menus, menu boards, or display cards.[45] Instances of mislabeling also include imported farmed salmon being falsely identified as wild Alaska salmon,[46] frozen seafood being marketed as fresh product, and confusion over seafood being marketed as organic. In response to these reports, FDA began collecting samples from the wholesale distribution chain, prior to the point of final sale, and a limited amount of samples from the point of import.[47] When compared to the FDA's Seafood List, a guide to acceptable market and common names for imported seafood and seafood sold in interstate commerce, 15% of the samples were found to be incorrectly labeled.

Fraud can be perpetrated in a variety of ways and at different market levels. Problems can arise from substitution at the restaurant level, misrepresentation by the restaurant supplier, or product misidentification anywhere in the harvesting and processing system. It is often difficult to determine who may have been at fault, especially if there is collusion. Intentional fraud, rather than human error, is more likely to have occurred when cheaper species are consistently mislabeled as more valuable species, rather than the other way around. One study, based on an analysis of mitochondrial DNA sequences, revealed that 77% of the fish sold in the U.S. marketplace as red snapper, *Lutjanus campechanus*, belonged to other species of the Lutjanidae family. In these cases, identification of other snapper species as red snapper is illegal.[48] In another case, a seafood wholesaler in Alabama was convicted of selling Asian catfish and Lake Victoria perch as groupers, and farm-raised shrimp as wild-caught shrimp.[49]

Determining the Identity of Fish Species

Regulators and consumers are faced with the challenge of identifying fish species to detect substitution in the marketplace. Fish can be difficult to identify especially in fillet or other processed forms. Until recently FDA has depended on isoelectric focusing electrophoresis of soluble muscle proteins, a method that requires subjective interpretations of results and is not reliable for species identification of heat-processed or dried fish products.[50]

Each species of fish has a unique DNA sequence, sometimes referred to as a *barcode*. Scientists can accurately determine the identity of a species by testing DNA from small samples of its flesh. The Fish Barcode of Life is a collaborative international effort that is establishing a reference library of DNA barcodes for fish species.[51] Since 2007, FDA and the Smithsonian Institution have been developing DNA identification methods for regulatory use. FDA has developed methods and standards that are consistent across FDA laboratories and compiled a website of DNA barcodes for common seafood items. The website provides data for 411 species, with scientific names, DNA sequences, and photographs of most specimens.[52] Fish now can be sampled and compared to reference samples in the library to confirm their identity. The costs of identification have fallen significantly as DNA techniques have been refined and the costs of DNA-sequencing equipment have fallen. FDA now performs these tests in many of its regional field laboratories as part of investigations related to seafood fraud.

Because large quantities of seafood are imported for U.S. consumption, some portion of the mislabeling problem undoubtedly originates with foreign suppliers. To address this concern FDA has issued an import alert on species substitution to provide guidance to agency field personnel about the manufacturers and/or products at issue.[53] Asian catfish (basa and tra) may illustrate the magnitude of the problem. Although import volumes exceed 50 million pounds annually for these species, they sometimes are identified incorrectly in the domestic marketplace. For example, in 2012, a California seafood corporation was fined $1 million for selling Asian catfish as grouper.[54]

Common Names of Fish

Although species substitution may be intentional for certain species and products because of their differing values, it also occurs unintentionally because the identities of species are easily mistaken. *Table 1* provides a list of some common illegally substituted species. Common names such as red snapper are sometimes used for a variety of different species both unintentionally and intentionally.

Table 1. Examples of Common Illegally Substituted Seafood (less expensive products are in column B)

A	B
Red Snapper	Pacific Rockfish
Red Snapper	Various Snappers
Mahi Mahi	Yellowtail (Seriola lalandi)
Swordfish	Mako Shark
Orange Roughy	Oreo Dory or John Dory
Cod	Alaska Pollock
Halibut	Sea Bass
Dover Sole	Arrowtooth Flounder
Red Drum	Black Drum
Snapper (Lutjanus sp.) Grouper Lake or Yellow Perch	Tilapia Basa or Tra White Perch or Zander
Caviar (sturgeon species) Walleye Chum Salmon	Paddlefish or Other Fish Roe Sauger or Alaska Pollock Pink Salmon
Salmon	Steelhead Trout
Blue Crab Meat	Imported Crab Meat
Wild-Caught Salmon	Farm-Raised Salmon

Source: Food and Drug Administration (FDA), FDA's Examples of Substituted Seafood, at http://www.fda.gov/ Food/FoodScienceResearch/RFE/ ucm071528.htm.

The two main provisions that cover the naming of fish are Section 403 of FFDCA, which addresses misbranded food, and Title 21, Section 102.5, of the *Code of Federal Regulations*, which sets forth general principles for common or usual names for non-standardized food. FDA recognizes the acceptable market name as the appropriate label for seafood products in interstate commerce. The acceptable market name "is a name that FDA recognizes as a suitable statement of identity in labeling a species" and fairly represents the identity to consumers. The use of vernacular names is discouraged because a species may have different vernacular names in different regions and because different species may be called by the same vernacular name. A common or usual name is the "prevalent and meaningful name by which consumers ordinarily identify the food."[55] Often the common name and acceptable market name are the same. For example, sablefish, *Anoplopoma fimbri,* has the same market and common name. If they are not misleading, FDA generally regards common names as appropriate seafood names.

The Seafood List

The term *seafood* includes an exceptionally large number and variety of species. In 1988, FDA and NOAA developed its Seafood List. In addition to serving as a guide to acceptable market and common names, the list can be used as a standard reference to reduce confusion among consumers and provides an authoritative source for processors, retailers, and other vendors.[56] FDA's guidance documents are recommendations, and thus the Seafood List does not establish legally enforceable requirements. In 1993, FDA published an updated and expanded Seafood List to include invertebrate species (mollusks and crustaceans) as well as finfish. The list is updated every six months and includes the following display for each species:

- type (vertebrate, invertebrate, crustacean);
- acceptable market name (e.g. grouper);
- common name (e.g. red grouper); and
- scientific name (e.g. *Epinephelus morio*)

The list includes 1,827 seafood species and species groups, 1,737 common names, and 555 market names for seafood items.[57] Often the acceptable market name is more general than the more specific common name. For example, there are 47 different species listed with the market name of grouper, all of which have different common names. In this case, one market name may be used for a number of different grouper species. Use of either the acceptable market name or the common name assures seafood venders that their labeling of seafood will comply with FDA regulations. In contrast, for some species such as red snapper, market names are required by regulation. The labeling or sale of any fish other than *Lutjanus campechanus* as red snapper constitutes a misbranding in violation of FFDCA.[58]

Recent state efforts in California illustrated the difficulties related to using common and market names. In August 2014, the California legislature passed S.B. 1138 to address the problem of seafood fraud. The bill would have required the labeling of all fish and shellfish by their common name and of whether a species is wild-caught or farm-raised.[59] Seafood industry representatives opposed the bill. They claimed it would have generated confusion and been difficult to enforce because of the large number of common names for seafood. Governor Jerry Brown supported the intent of the measure but vetoed the bill. The governor stated that species-specific labeling of seafood would not be achieved easily and that the legislation would have created uncertainties and complexities that would have been difficult to resolve.[60]

Low Weights, Undercounting, and Overtreating

Consumers or businesses in the seafood supply chain receive less product for their money than advertised and anticipated when seafood businesses employ inaccurate (low) counts or net weights (*short-weighting*) and overtreatment.[61] These practices also constitute mislabeling offenses under FFDCA. Some businesses resort to these practices because the chances of being caught may be low and it makes their products appear relatively inexpensive and increases profits, at least in the short run.

The FDA standard for breaded shrimp requires that such a product contain at least 50% shrimp. Overbreading may cause consumers to pay shrimp prices for excess bread crumbs. Frozen fillets, shrimp, crab legs, and other products normally are protected from dehydration (freezer burn) with the application of a light glaze of ice. Excessive amounts of glaze (over-glazing) that are not accounted for can be used deliberately to increase the apparent weight, and therefore the apparent value, of the delivered product. On February 20, 2009, FDA reissued its 1991 guidance, warning the seafood industry that the net weight of frozen seafood may not include the weight of glazing and that violations of this kind may be criminally prosecuted as felonies.[62] Recent comments submitted to the presidential task force on combating IUU fishing and seafood fraud by the Southern Shrimp Alliance stated that greater efforts are needed to stop short-weighting of seafood products.[63]

The seafood industry uses sodium tripolyphosphate (STPP) to retain moisture in products so as to prevent freezer burn. When properly used, STPP can be a legitimate means for aiding processing and maintaining product quality. However, STPP can be misused to retain excess moisture in seafood products. For example, Atlantic sea scallops or shrimp may absorb excessive water after prolonged soaking in an STPP-water solution. Such excess water misrepresents the product's total weight and value when seafood prices are charged for the extra water. In addition to paying for excess water, shrimp can be bumped to a higher weight class (lower count per pound), which can increase the price per pound. Seafood treated with STPP or other water-retaining chemicals must be accurately labeled to identify this treatment. However, FDA rescinded moisture-percentage requirements in 2004 and now only requires that additives be listed on labels. NOAA's seafood inspection handbook assumes that scallops with a moisture content of greater than 83% have been treated and should be properly labeled as such.[64] No moisture guidelines or standards exist for shrimp. Some critics suggest that the use of all water-retention chemicals (primarily phosphates) should be prohibited in fish and shellfish.

Altered Color

Fish fillets can be treated with carbon monoxide (CO) to give fish flesh a fresher-appearing reddish tint. The growing use of CO (also referred to as *tasteless smoke* or TS) as a pigment fixative has alarmed some consumer advocates who say it deceives shoppers who depend on color to help them avoid spoiled fish. Seafood industry representatives assert that TS/CO is a legitimate preservative, and FDA has responded that it has no questions at this time regarding an industry determination that TS/CO is a substance *generally recognized as safe* (GRAS).[65] However, FDA has not made its own determination as to whether TS/CO is GRAS. A seafood safety concern occurs when the flesh of certain species, such as tuna, develops toxic levels of histamine through time and/or temperature abuse. Some assert that CO treatment may mask visual cues indicating that such flesh is decomposed and toxic. Consumer advocates have urged FDA to conduct a formal evaluation of this treatment's impact on consumer safety.[66] FDA considers tuna to be misbranded if it is treated with TS/CO but not labeled to indicate that it contains a preservative and thus purports to be unprocessed, fresh, or fresh-frozen tuna.[67]

Some aquaculture operations use color additives such as canthaxanthin or astaxanthin in feed to impart a more orange color to fish flesh of salmon or trout.[68] If not for these color additives, the flesh of the farmed varieties of these fish would be a possibly less appealing, paler color. Under specified conditions, use of these additives in feed for salmonid fish is legal as long as fish are properly labeled to identify that this treatment has been used.[69]

Transshipment and Mislabeling to Avoid Customs Duties

Transshipment occurs when foreign producers ship goods through a second country en route to the United States. Although transshipment is generally legal and commonly used in the ordinary course of business, it is illegal if done for the purpose of circumventing duties and other applicable trade restrictions. For example, shrimp from China reportedly have been shipped to the United States by way of Cambodia and Malaysia to avoid paying antidumping duties levied by the United States on shrimp imported from China.[70] In other cases, seafood such as Asian catfish has been mislabeled as sole specifically to avoid paying antidumping duties.[71]

Mislabeling the country of origin is another example of fraud. Without labeling, consumers rarely would be able to distinguish a product's country of origin. For example, some businesses may falsely claim their seafood product is domestic when it is actually imported from another country. Particularly for seafood, some difficult questions are related to the meaning of the term *country of origin*. For example, is a product's origin best represented by where the seafood was caught, the flag of the harvesting vessel, where the harvest was first landed, where the product was first processed, or where it was last or secondarily processed?[72] Some consumers and businesses have become more interested in tracing seafood throughout the supply chain so the source of and liability for any mislabeling can be more easily identified.[73]

TRACEABILITY OF SEAFOOD

During the last several decades, international seafood trade and movement of seafood throughout the United States have increased. Most seafood is no longer obtained from local sources; more than 90% of seafood consumed in

United States is imported.[74] This shift has led to greater industry and consumer interest in tracing seafood throughout the supply chain from fishing vessel or aquaculture operation to the final consumer. The Bioterrorism Act of 2002 (P.L. 107-188) requires producers, distributers, importers, transporters, and packers to maintain records of the sources and recipients of its products, or one step forward and one step back in the supply chain.[75] The law also requires businesses to make these records available to FDA when there is a reasonable belief that adulterated food presents a threat of serious adverse health consequences or death to humans or animals.

Seafood traceability can be used to identify, locate, and withdraw harmful products from stores and restaurants. Traceability of products also can identify where fraud occurs in the supply chain or detect seafood products obtained from IUU activities. Consumers are becoming more concerned with product quality, identity, and sustainability. Currently, most seafood businesses do not provide information such as where, how, and when a specific seafood item was caught. Some fisheries are certified as sustainable by nongovernmental organizations and labeled as such to convey this information to consumers. For certified products, traceability through the supply chain is required to confirm the origin and identity of seafood products.

Some segments of the fishing industry believe that adopting systems to trace products from "capture to plate" can improve profits. Tracking requires tagging fish at the time of capture and recording related information such has vessel, date, species, weight, and location of capture at the time of unloading. This information is linked to products as barcodes or tags as they move through the supply chain. Because fish are a perishable commodity, the ability to quickly identify products and their location can improve efficiency and decrease waste. Traceability also can improve customer service by providing the capacity to quickly identify and correct problems when they occur.

Whether similar information should be required for all seafood items and markets remains an open question. Broad adoption of seafood tracing systems would require universal standards and information from across businesses in the supply chain. Although more information could decrease costs associated with seafood fraud and potentially improve efficiency, these gains would need to be weighed against potential costs of developing and maintaining the traceability system.

LOSSES ASSOCIATED WITH SEAFOOD FRAUD

There are no estimates of total economic losses associated with seafood fraud, but costs to consumers and legitimate seafood business likely are substantial. When seafood products are short-weighted, the losses to the buyer or consumer are in proportion to the difference between the labeled and actual weights. In 2012, U.S. consumers spent $82.6 billion for seafood products, which includes $55.2 billion in expenditures at food service establishments and $26.8 billion in retail sales for home consumption.[76] When paying for excess water or breadcrumbs, consumers may sustain direct losses in proportion to the excess filler used to increase the weight of the product. The National Institute of Standards and Technology speculated that if only 2% of the weight of all seafood is short-weighted, the annual loss to consumers could be as high as $1.6 billion.[77]

Consumers may incur losses when purchasing a lower-valued substitute for the price of a higher-valued product. They also may gain less utility from consuming a product of lower quality even when they are unaware of whether substitution has taken place. Consumers may find inferior substitutes to be less desirable and factor this experience into future food purchases. It is not clear whether the amount of fraud and deception in seafood sales and marketing is increasing, but media and nongovernmental organization attention to this issue has raised its profile with the public. These reports may deter consumers from purchasing seafood because of suspicions that they may not be getting the product they expect. Both consumer experiences and reports of seafood fraud may change consumer tastes and preferences for seafood products and decrease demand for seafood.

For example, a study of Floridians found that 62% of respondents were familiar with media reports of restaurants substituting lower-valued species for grouper.[78] Among respondents who were aware of the reports and order grouper at restaurants, 39% said they were less likely to purchase grouper at restaurants, 21% said they were less likely to purchase grouper for home consumption, 13% said they were less likely to order other types of fish at restaurants, and 9% said they were less likely to purchase other fish for home consumption. Study participants were willing to pay $0.83 to $3.18 more for grouper entrees in restaurants if these products were supplied with an integrity label.[79]

The seafood industry also is likely to sustain losses because of the lower consumer perception of its products and a related decrease in demand. A decrease in demand would result in lower prices and losses in revenue to law-abiding businesses. These businesses also compete with those selling fraudulent products for lower prices. Lower-priced substitutes, albeit fraudulent, can put downward pressure on prices for legitimate, high-quality products.

INDUSTRY INITIATIVES

In 1986, the Southeastern Fisheries Association introduced a Seafood Product Quality Code program—one of the first efforts by a fisheries trade association to inform wholesale and retail seafood buyers.[80] The code, a voluntary educational and promotional concept developed by the seafood industry, cataloged the industry's recommended measures for product quality of specific seafood products.[81] Each product, such as raw headless shrimp, is listed with a description of its characteristics, such as production method, product types, product forms, quality attributes, packaging, and labeling. The availability of this information was intended to increase quality and safety awareness and to improve communication between buyers and sellers.

In October 2006, concerns that seafood fraud had eroded consumer confidence in seafood led the National Fisheries Institute (NFI) to announce an initiative to promote economic integrity within the seafood industry. NFI officially launched its Better Seafood Bureau in July 2007.[82]Implementation of this initiative identified three primary concerns:

- transshipment of products to avoid antidumping and countervailing duties;
- mislabeling of products or species substitution; and
- mislabeling of weights or counts of products.

NFI is pursuing its initiative by obtaining commitments from the CEOs of NFI member companies to comply with industry principles of economic integrity and to report suppliers committing economic fraud.[83] As part of its economic integrity initiative, NFI reported that, in the year ending in August 2008, it sent more than 80 letters to FDA documenting specific examples of fraudulent weights.

However, NFI has not been an advocate for new seafood fraud laws. NFI has maintained that "FDA needs to fulfill its mandate to fight seafood fraud" and "enforce laws that are already on the books."[84] It contends that calling for new laws suggests some advocacy groups do not understand the issue. NFI adds that its "members have been aggressive in rooting out bad actors and pushing regulators to enforce laws designed to stop this type of activity."[85] In 2013, NFI and the National Restaurant Association signed an MOU to join forces in the fight against seafood fraud.[86]

ADMINISTRATION INITIATIVE

On June 17, 2014, President Obama released a presidential memorandum entitled— "Comprehensive Framework to Combat Illegal, Unreported, and Unregulated Fishing and Seafood Fraud."[87] The memorandum called on executive departments and agencies to use existing authorities to combat IUU fishing and seafood fraud. The memorandum also established a task force composed of senior-level federal agency representatives to develop recommendations for a comprehensive framework that targets IUU fishing and seafood fraud. On March 15, 2015, the task force released its final recommendations, which included both international and domestic measures.[88] The task force's 15 recommendations are organized according to the following categories:

International: Work with international governments, regional fisheries management organizations, and others to combat IUU fishing and seafood fraud at the international level.

Enforcement: Strengthen enforcement tools to combat IUU fishing.

Partnership: Create and expand partnerships with U.S. state and local governments, industry, and nongovernmental organizations to identify and eliminate seafood fraud and IUU seafood in U.S. commerce.

Traceability: Create a risk-based traceability program to track seafood from harvest to entry into U.S. commerce to prevent entry of illegal product into the supply chain and better inform retailers and consumers.

The National Ocean Council has been changed with establishing an IUU Fishing and Seafood Fraud Committee to coordinate implementation of the task force's recommendations.[89]

IUU fishing occurs throughout the world, and a significant portion of seafood entering the United States reportedly is obtained from IUU fishing activities. Although IUU fishing may be a significant problem, some have questioned whether IUU fishing and seafood fraud should be addressed as part of the same initiative.[90] Those who harvest seafood illegally may attempt to avoid detection by concealing its origin or mislabeling seafood, but seafood fraud can occur whether seafood products are harvested legally or illegally. Some have recommended that IUU fishing needs to be addressed at the source, before the product enters the market system. In contrast, seafood fraud may occur at different points in the supply chain and needs to be addressed accordingly. Furthermore, some explain that the terms *seafood fraud* and *IUU* are being used very broadly and question whether they need to be redefined or categorized to address specific types of illegal activity.[91]

GAO Seafood Fraud Report and Agency Coordination

In February 2009, the Government Accountability Office (GAO) released a report on seafood fraud that focused on the federal government's role in addressing this problem.[92] GAO concluded that federal agencies have not taken advantage of opportunities to share information that could benefit individual agency efforts to detect and prevent seafood fraud, and have not identified similar and sometimes overlapping activities that could be better coordinated to use limited resources more efficiently. The reported concluded that the lack of collaboration among Customs and Border Patrol, National Marine Fisheries Service (NOAA), and FDA has resulted in overlapping actions and inefficient use of resources.

According to GAO, FDA has considered detection of seafood fraud-related violations to be a low priority and has devoted minimal resources to this activity.[93] At the time of GAO's study in 2009, FDA program guidance to field staff stated that "no resources have been allocated for seafood fraud-related work, and resource expenditures in this area should be kept to a minimum."[94] FDA officials stated that, "the agency does not have the staff or resources to address economic fraud in addition to their food safety responsibilities."[95] Since GAO released its report in 2009, FDA has dedicated resources to improving DNA testing for seafood fraud, collecting data related to the occurrence of seafood fraud, and launching an online training module related to seafood fraud.[96]

GAO also questioned whether seafood safety requirements of FDA's Hazard Analysis Critical Control Point (HACCP) regulations should include seafood fraud. Under HACCP, domestic processors are required to prepare site- and product-specific plans that analyze potential safety hazards, identify where possible hazards occur during processing, monitor hazard control points, and determine how hazards will be controlled. Importers of seafood produced in other countries also must take steps to verify that the products obtained from foreign processors are in compliance with HACCP rules. When HACCP regulations were developed in 1995, FDA also proposed guidelines for using an HACCP-based approach to control economic fraud under FFDCA. However, measures related to economic fraud were not included in the HACCP regulations that FDA adopted for seafood safety. FDA explained that the food system would need to mature before the agency should address matters other than food safety. GAO recommended FDA propose changes to its HACCP regulations to include requirements for identifying and mitigating economic fraud risks.[97]

On October 9, 2009, NOAA and FDA concluded an MOU to improve cooperation and information sharing in the inspection of seafood products and establishments.[98] The arrangement attempts to address the GAO recommendations by strengthening the agencies' partnership and outlines procedures to work together both at headquarters and in the field. The MOU recognizes that FDA may take NOAA inspections into account when establishing inspection priorities. The MOU represents a broad outline of the parties' intent to collaborate in areas of mutual interest, but it did not create binding and enforceable obligations for either agency.

End Notes

[1] National Oceanic and Atmospheric Administration (NOAA), FishWatch: U.S. Seafood Facts, "Combating Seafood Fraud: Regulators and Industry Unite," at http://www.fishwatch.gov/buying_seafood/combating_seafood_fraud.htm. NOAA administers a voluntary seafood inspection program.

[2] Kirk Johnson, "Survey Finds That Fish Are Often Not What Label Says," New York Times, February 21, 2013.

[3] NOAA, FishWatch: U.S. Seafood Facts, "Identifying Seafood Fraud: A Common Practice with Serious Consequences," at http://www.fishwatch.gov/buying_ seafood/ identifying_ seafood_fraud.htm.

[4] Consumers may include any buyers in the market chain such as wholesalers, retail markets, and food service establishments.

[5] Jann Th. Martinsohn, Deterring Illegal Activities in the Fisheries Sector: Genetics, Genomics, Chemistry and Forensics to Fight IUU Fishing and in Support of Fish Product Traceability, European Commission Joint Research Centre (JRC), JRC Reference Report, 2011.

[6] The White House, Office of the Press Secretary, "Presidential Memorandum—Comprehensive Framework to Combat Illegal, Unreported, and Unregulated Fishing and Seafood Fraud," press release, June 17, 2014, at http://www.whitehouse.gov/the-press-office/2014/06/17/presidential-memorandum-comprehensive-frameworkcombat-illegal-unreporte.

[7] Presidential Task Force on Combating IUU Fishing and Seafood Fraud, Action Plan for Implementing the Task Force Recommendations, March 2015.

[8] John Sackton, "Industry urges feds IUU and Seafood Fraud Task Force to keep the two issues separate," Seafood News, September 2, 2014.

[9] This bill was similar to H.R. 1012 and S. 520, which were introduced during the 113th Congress.

[10] For a broader discussion of food fraud, see CRS Report R43358, Food Fraud and "Economically Motivated Adulteration" of Food and Food Ingredients, by Renée Johnson.

[11] Most meat and poultry are inspected by the United States Department of Agriculture's Food Safety Inspection Service.

[12] Committee on State Food Labeling, Institute of Medicine, Food Labeling Toward National Uniformity, ed. Donna V. Porter and Robert O. Earl (Washington, DC: National Academies Press, 1992).

[13] 21 U.S.C. §341.

[14] 21 U.S.C. §343(a). The Food and Drug Administration (FDA) further regulates this area of misbranding in 21 C.F.R. §101.18.

[15] 21 U.S.C. §342 (b)(2).

[16] 15 U.S.C. §1453(a).

[17] 15 U.S.C. §1451.

[18] 15 U.S.C. §1452.

[19] 15 U.S.C. §1456(a).

[20] 21 C.F.R. §102.5(a).

[21] 21 C.F.R. §102.5(d).

[22] 21 C.F.R. §102.46.

[23] FDA is an agency in the Department of Health and Human Services.

[24] The U.S. Department of Agriculture (USDA) is implementing an inspection program for catfish.

[25] FDA, "Seafood Guidance Documents & Regulatory Information," at http://www.fda.gov/Food/GuidanceRegulation/GuidanceDocumentsRegulatoryInformation/Seafood/default.htm.

[26] CRS Report R43794, Food Recalls and Other FDA Administrative Enforcement Actions, by Emily M. Lanza and CRS Report R43927, Food Safety Issues: FDA Judicial Enforcement Actions, by Emily M. Lanza.

[27] Violative product means the product or condition does not comply with laws and regulations enforced by FDA.

[28] The Department of Justice represents FDA and the federal government in judicial proceedings.

[29] Customs and Border Protection is an agency in the Department of Homeland Security.

[30] The act also makes exemptions if articles are incapable of being marked or the cost would be economically prohibitive. Another set of exceptions is the "J List," named for section 1304(a)(3)(J), which in certain cases exempts specified products from labeling requirements, including fish.

[31] 19 U.S.C. §1592.

[32] The program is sometimes identified as the Department of Commerce or National Marine Fisheries Seafood Inspection Program. The Seafood Inspection Program is part of the National Marine Fisheries Service (NMFS) line office within NOAA which is an agency in the Department of Commerce.

[33] For example, see U.S. Department of Justice (DOJ), "Two Found Guilty of Conspiracy Involving the Importation and Sale of Falsely Labeled Fish from Vietnam," press release, October 30, 2008, at http://www.justice.gov/opa/pr/ 2008/October/08-enrd-967.html.

[34] For example, see U.S. Attorney's Office, "Fish Processor Sentenced to Prison for Selling Falsely Labeled Salmon," press release, April 1, 2011, at http://www.justice.gov/ usao/waw/ press/2011/apr/jay.html.

[35] NOAA, "NOAA Investigations into Mislabeling Seafood Protects Consumers and Fishermen," press release, February 4, 2011, at http://www.noaanews.noaa.gov/ stories 2011/20110204_seafoodmislabeling.html.

[36] CRS Report RS22955, Country-of-Origin Labeling for Foods and the WTO Trade Dispute on Meat Labeling, by Joel L. Greene

[37] 7 C.F.R. Part 60; See USDA, "Mandatory Country of Origin Labeling of Fish and Shellfish," 69 Federal Register 59708-59750, October 5, 2004.

[38] 7 C.F.R. §60.105 and 7 C.F.R. §60.119.

[39] USDA, "Mandatory Country of Origin Labeling of Beef, Pork, Lamb, Chicken, Goat, Meat, Wild and Farm-Raised Fish and Shellfish, Perishable Agricultural Commodities, Peanuts, Pecans, Ginseng, and Macadamia Nuts," 74 Federal Register 2658-2707, January 15, 2009.

[40] The family Ictaluridae includes North American catfish and is one of 36 families in the order Siluriformes, which also includes Asian catfish. Most catfish raised and imported from Asia are Siluriformes.

[41] USDA, FSIS, "Mandatory Inspection of Catfish and Catfish Products," 76 Federal Register 10434-10467, February 24, 2011.

[42] Alaska Stat. §17.20.045.

[43] California Business and Professions Code §12024.

[44] "Mystery Fish," Consumer Reports Magazine, December 2011, at http://www. consumer reports.org/cro/magazinearchive/2011/december/food/fake-fish/overview/index.htm.

[45] Jonathan E. Fielding, Director and Health Officer, Mislabeled Seafood Sold in Restaurants and Grocery Stores Overview, County of Los Angeles Public Health, Los Angeles, CA, November 1, 2012.

[46] For an Alaskan perspective on seafood fraud, see Barb Cooper, "Fish Faking," Alaska, vol. 77, no. 10 (December 2011/January 2012), pp. 32-42.

[47] FDA, Summary of FDA's sampling efforts for seafood species labeling in FY12-13, College Park, MD, September 2013, at http://www.fda.gov/downloads/Food/Guidance Regulation/ GuidanceDocumentsRegulatoryInformation/ Seafood/UCM419983.pdf.

[48] P. B. Marko et al., "Fisheries: Mislabeling of a Depleted Reef Fish," Nature, vol. 430 (July 2004), pp. 309-310. FDA policy states that labeling or sale of any fish other than Lutjanus campechanus as red snapper constitutes a misbranding in violation of the Federal Food Drug and Cosmetic Act of 1938 (FFDCA; 21 U.S.C. §§301 et seq.)

[49] U.S. Department of Justice, "Seafood Wholesaler Owners Sentenced in Alabama for Selling Falsely Labeled Fish, Smuggling and Misbranding Seafood Products," press release, May 5, 2011, at http://www.justice.gov/opa/pr/2011/ May/11-enrd-577.html.

[50] FDA, "DNA-based Seafood Identification," at http://www.fda.gov/food/foodscienceresearch/ dnaseafoodidentification/default.htm.

[51] International Barcode of Life, FDA using barcoding to spot fish fraud, Barcode Bulletin, March 2012, at http://ibol.org/fda-using-barcoding-to-spot-fish-fraud/.

[52] FDA, "Vertebrates: Reference Standard Sequence Library for Seafood Identification," at http://www.fda.gov/Food/FoodScienceResearch/DNASeafoodIdentification/ucm238880.htm.

[53] FDA, Import Alert 16-04, Misbranded Seafood, January 7, 2014, at http://www. acces sdata.fda.gov/cms_ia/ importalert_13.html

[54] NOAA, FishWatch: U.S. Seafood Facts, "Combating Seafood Fraud," at http://www.fishwatch.gov/buying_seafood/ combating_seafood_fraud.htm.

[55] 63 Fed. Reg. 20,148 (April 23, 1998).

[56] FDA, "The Seafood List," at http://www.accessdata.fda.gov/scripts/fdcc/?set=seafoodlist.

[57] For some species and species groups, a common name is not provided, but all species and species groups have a market name.

[58] FDA, "Inspections, Compliance, Enforcement, and Criminal Investigations," Sec. 540.475 (Snapper—Labeling) in Manual of Compliance Policy Guides.

[59] S.B.-1138 Fish and shellfish: labeling and identification, enrolled September 03, 2014, at http://leginfo.legislature.ca.gov/faces/billNavClient.xhtml?bill_id=201320140SB1138.

[60] Alexei Coseff, "Jerry Brown Vetoes Seafood Labeling Bill," Sacramento Bee, September 30, 2014.

[61] For more background on this practice, see James Wright, "The Weighting Game: The Seafood Industry Addresses Short-Weighting with Little Assistance," Seafood Business, July 2009, at http://www.seafoodbusiness.com/ articledetail.aspx?id=4294994041.

[62] FDA, "Guidance for Industry: 1991 Letter to Seafood Manufacturers Regarding the Fraudulent Practice of Including Glaze (ice) as Part of the Weight of Frozen Seafood," February 2009, at http://www.fda.gov/Food/GuidanceRegulation/GuidanceDocumentsRegulatory Information/Seafood/ucm123018.htm.

[63] Letter from John Williams, Executive Director, Southern Shrimp Alliance, to Laurel Bryant, Chief of External Affairs, National Marine Fisheries Service, September 2, 2014, at http://www.shrimpalliance.com/wp-content/uploads/ 2014/09/SSA-comments-on-Presidents-Task-Force-on-IUU-and-seafood-fraud-9-2-14.pdf.

[64] NOAA, Seafood Inspection Program, Inspection Manual 25, (Silver Spring, MD: 2011), p. 91.

[65] Letter from Janice F. Oliver, Deputy Director, Center for Food Safety and Applied Nutrition, FDA, to Martin J. Hahn, Hogan and Hartson L.L.P., March 10, 2000, at http://www.fda.gov/Food/IngredientsPackagingLabeling/GRAS/ NoticeInventory/ucm154892.htm.

[66] U.S. Congress, House Committee on Energy and Commerce, Subcommittee on Oversight and Investigations, Statement by Dr. David Acheson, Associate Commissioner on Foods, FDA, Recent Food Safety Activities at the Food and Drug Administration, 110th Cong., 1st sess., November 13, 2007.

[67] U.S. Department of Commerce, NOAA, USDC Verified Facilities of Fishery Products Treated with Carbon Monoxide and Filtered Smoke Gas, Seafood Inspection Program, October 21, 2003, at http://seafood.oregonstate.edu/.pdf%20Links/USDC-Verified-Facilities-of-Fishery-Products-Treated-with-Carbon-Monoxide-and-Filtered-SmokeGas.pdf.

[68] Fereidoon Shahidi, Metusalach, and Joseph A. Brown, "Carotenoid Pigments in Seafoods and Aquaculture," Critical Reviews in Food Science and Nutrition, vol. 28, no. 1 (1998): 1-67.

[69] 21 C.F.R. §73.35; 21 C.F.R. §73.75.

[70] Department of Commerce, "Administrative Review of Certain Frozen Warmwater Shrimp From the People's Republic of China," 77 Federal Register 53856-53862, September 4, 2012. U.S. Congress, House Committee on Ways and Means, Subcommittee on Trade, Supporting Economic Growth and Job Creation Through Customs Trade Modernization, Facilitation, and Enforcement, 112th Cong., May 17, 2012.

[71] NOAA, "NOAA Investigations Into Mislabeling Seafood Protects Consumers and Fishermen," press release, February 4, 2011, at http://www.noaanews.noaa.gov/stories 2011/20110204_seafoodmislabeling.html.

[72] For example, some seafood products such as pink salmon are harvested in Alaska, shipped to China for processing, and exported from China to the United States.

[73] Ami Petersen and David Green, Seafood Traceability: A Practical Guide for the U.S. Industry, North Carolina Sea Grant, Report UNC-SG-06-04, 28 p.; at http://www.ncseagrant.org/files/seafood_traceability.pdf.

[74] NOAA, FishWatch: U.S. Seafood Facts, "Outside the U.S.," at http://www.fishwatch.gov/farmed_seafood/ outside_the_us.htm.

[75] National Fisheries Institute, U.S. Seafood Traceability Implementation Guide, Issue 1.1, March 2011.

[76] National Marine Fisheries Service, Fisheries of the United States 2012, (Silver Spring, MD: September 2013), at http://www.st.nmfs.noaa.gov/Assets/commercial/fus/ fus12/ 01_front2012.pdf.

[77] David Sefcik, "Seafood Fraud - Where Are We Now?," Weights and Measures Connections, vol. 2, no. 7 (December 11, 2011).

[78] Andrew J. Ropicki, Sherry Larkin, and Charles Adams, "Seafood Substitution and Mislabeling: WTP for a Locally Caught Grouper Labeling Program in Florida," Marine Resource Economics, vol. 25, no. 1 (2010), pp. 77-92. Hereinafter cited as Ropicki et al. 2010.

[79] The survey stated that the integrity label would guarantee the fish is fresh grouper caught in Florida. Ropicki et al. 2010.

[80] The program was funded under a Saltonstall-Kennedy Act grant.

[81] Southeastern Fisheries Association, Seafood Product Quality Code, 2000, at http://seafood.oregonstate.edu/.pdf%20Links/Seafood-Product-Qaulity-Code.pdf.

[82] The name was officially changed to the Better Seafood Board in May 2009 to avoid confusion with the Better Business Bureau.

[83] Better Seafood Board, "About the Better Seafood Board," at http://www.aboutseafood.com/about/about-nfi/betterseafood-board.

[84] National Fisheries Institute, "National Fisheries Institute Says FDA Should Enforce Seafood Fraud Laws, Congress Need Not Pass New Ones," press release, February 20, 2013, at http://www.aboutseafood.com/press/press-releases/ media-alert-4.

[85] Ibid.

[86] National Fisheries Institute, "Trade Associations Sign MOU Aimed at Quashing Dishonest Practices," press release, September 23, 2013, at http://www.aboutseafood.com/press/press-releases/nfi-nra-fight-seafood-fraud-menumislabeling.

[87] The White House, Office of the Press Secretary, "Presidential Memorandum—Comprehensive Framework to Combat Illegal, Unreported, and Unregulated Fishing and Seafood Fraud," press release, June 17, 2014, at http://www.whitehouse.gov/the-press-office/2014/06/17/presidential-memorandum-comprehensive-frameworkcombat-illegal-unreporte.

[88] Presidential Task Force on Combating IUU Fishing and Seafood Fraud, Action Plan for Implementing the Task Force Recommendations, March 2015.

[89] The National Ocean Council (NOC) was established by E.O. 13547 to implement the National Ocean Policy. Membership of the NOC includes the secretaries of most federal departments and other high-ranking officials who have responsibilities related to ocean management.

[90] John Sackton, "Industry urges feds IUU and Seafood Fraud Task Force to keep the two issues separate," Seafood News, September 2, 2014.

[91] For the IUU fishing definition in NMFS regulations, see 50 C.F.R §300.201.

[92] U.S. Government Accountability Office, Seafood Fraud: FDA Program Changes and Better Collaboration among Key Federal Agencies Could Improve Detection and Prevention, February 2009, GAO-09-258, 49 p.

93 Ibid., p. 13.

[94] Ibid., p. 18.

[95] Ibid., p. 18.

[96] Christine Blank, "FDA seafood fraud investigation finds fewer offenses," Seafood Source, October 27, 2014.

[97] GAO 2009, p. 31.

[98] FDA and NOAA, "Memorandum of Understanding Between U.S. Department of Commerce National Oceanic and Atmospheric Administration and U.S. Department of Health and Human Services Food and Drug Administration," October 2009.

INDEX

A

B

C

D

E

F

G

H

I

J

K

L

M

N

O

P

R

S